The **Essential** Buyer's Guide

# MORGAN
# PLUS 8

All models 1968 to 2004

Your marque expert:
Phil Benfield

**VELOCE PUBLISHING**
THE PUBLISHER OF FINE AUTOMOTIVE BOOKS

The Essential Buyer's Guide Series

Alfa Romeo Alfasud (Metcalfe)
Alfa Romeo Alfetta: all saloon/sedan models 1972 to 1984 & coupé models 1974 to 1987 (Metcalfe)
Alfa Romeo Giulia GT Coupé (Booker)
Alfa Romeo Giulia Spider (Booker)
Audi TT (Davies)
Audi TT Mk2 2006 to 2014 (Durnan)
Austin-Healey Big Healeys (Trummel)
BMW Boxer Twins (Henshaw)
BMW E30 3 Series 1981 to 1994 (Hosier)
BMW GS (Henshaw)
BMW X5 (Saunders)
BMW Z3 Roadster (Fishwick)
BMW Z4: E85 Roadster and E86 Coupé including M and Alpina 2003 to 2009 (Smitheram)
BSA 350, 441 & 500 Singles (Henshaw)
BSA 500 & 650 Twins (Henshaw)
BSA Bantam (Henshaw)
Choosing, Using & Maintaining Your Electric Bicycle (Henshaw)
Citroën 2CV (Paxton)
Citroën DS & ID (Heilig)
Cobra Replicas (Ayre)
Corvette C2 Sting Ray 1963-1967 (Falconer)
Datsun 240Z 1969 to 1973 (Newlyn)
DeLorean DMC-12 1981 to 1983 (Williams)
Ducati Bevel Twins (Falloon)
Ducati Desmodue Twins (Falloon)
Ducati Desmoquattro Twins – 851, 888, 916, 996, 998, ST4 1988 to 2004 (Falloon)
FIAT 124 Spider & Pininfarina Azzura Spider, (AS-DS) 1966 to 1985 (Robertson)
Fiat 500 & 600 (Bobbitt)
Ford Capri (Paxton)
Ford Escort Mk1 & Mk2 (Williamson)
Ford Focus Mk1 RS & ST170, 1st Generation (Williamson)
Ford Model A – All Models 1927 to 1931 (Buckley)
Ford Model T – All models 1909 to 1927 (Barker)
Ford Mustang – First Generation 1964 to 1973 (Cook)
Ford Mustang – 3rd generation: 1979-1993; inc Mercury Capri: 1979-1986 (Smith)
Ford Mustang – Fifth Generation (2005-2014) (Cook)
Ford RS Cosworth Sierra & Escort (Williamson)
Harley-Davidson Big Twins (Henshaw)
Hillman Imp (Morgan)
Hinckley Triumph triples & fours 750, 900, 955, 1000, 1050, 1200 – 1991-2009 (Henshaw)
Honda CBR FireBlade (Henshaw)
Honda CBR600 Hurricane (Henshaw)
Honda SOHC Fours 1969-1984 (Henshaw)
Jaguar E-type 3.8 & 4.2 litre (Crespin)
Jaguar E-type V12 5.3 litre (Crespin)
Jaguar Mark 1 & 2 (All models including Daimler 2.5-litre V8) 1955 to 1969 (Thorley)
Jaguar New XK 2005-2014 (Thorley)
Jaguar S-Type – 1999 to 2007 (Thorley)
Jaguar X-Type – 2001 to 2009 (Thorley)
Jaguar XJ-S (Crespin)
Jaguar XJ6, XJ8 & XJR (Thorley)
Jaguar XK 120, 140 & 150 (Thorley)
Jaguar XK8 & XKR (1996-2005) (Thorley)
Jaguar/Daimler XJ 1994-2003 (Crespin)
Jaguar/Daimler XJ40 (Crespin)
Jaguar/Daimler XJ6, XJ12 & Sovereign (Crespin)
Kawasaki Z1 & Z900 (Orritt)
Lancia Delta HF 4WD & Integrale (Baker)
Land Rover Discovery Series 1 (1989-1998) (Taylor)
Land Rover Discovery Series 2 (1998-2004) (Taylor)
Land Rover Series I, II & IIA (Thurman)
Land Rover Series III (Thurman)
Lotus Elan, S1 to Sprint and Plus 2 to Plus 2S 130/5 1962 to 1974 (Vale)
Lotus Europa, S1, S2, Twin-cam & Special 1966 to 1975 (Vale)
Lotus Seven replicas & Caterham 7: 1973-2013 (Hawkins)
Mazda MX-5 Miata (Mk1 1989-97 & Mk2 98-2001) (Crook)
Mazda MX-5 Miata (Mk3, 3.5 & 3.75 models, 2005-2015) (Wild)
Mazda RX-8 (Parish)

Mercedes-Benz 190: all 190 models (W201 series) 1982 to 1993 (Parish)
Mercedes-Benz 280-560SL & SLC (Bass)
Mercedes-Benz G-Wagen (Greene)
Mercedes-Benz Pagoda 230SL, 250SL & 280SL roadsters & coupés (Bass)
Mercedes-Benz S-Class W126 Series (Zoporowski)
Mercedes-Benz S-Class Second Generation W116 Series (Parish)
Mercedes-Benz SL R129-series 1989 to 2001 (Parish)
Mercedes-Benz SLK (Bass)
Mercedes-Benz W123 (Parish)
Mercedes-Benz W124 – All models 1984-1997 (Zoporowski)
MG Midget & A-H Sprite (Horler)
MG TD, TF & TF1500 (Jones)
MGA 1955-1962 (Crosier)
MGB & MGB GT (Williams)
MGF & MG TF (Hawkins)
Mini (Paxton)
Morgan 4/4 (Benfield)
Morgan Plus 4 (Benfield)
Morgan Plus 8 (Benfield)
Morris Minor & 1000 (Newell)
Moto Guzzi 2-valve big twins (Falloon)
New Mini (Collins)
Norton Commando (Henshaw)
Peugeot 205 GTI (Blackburn)
Piaggio Scooters – all modern two-stroke & four-stroke automatic models 1991 to 2016 (Willis)
Porsche 356 (Johnson)
Porsche 911 (964) (Streather)
Porsche 911 (991) (Streather)
Porsche 911 (993) (Streather)
Porsche 911 (996) (Streather)
Porsche 911 (997) – Model years 2004 to 2009 (Streather)
Porsche 911 (997) – Second generation models 2009 to 2012 (Streather)
Porsche 911 Carrera 3.2 (Streather)
Porsche 911SC (Streather)
Porsche 924 – All models 1976 to 1988 (Hodgkins)
Porsche 928 (Hemmings)
Porsche 930 Turbo & 911 (930) Turbo (Streather)
Porsche 944 (Higgins)
Porsche 981 Boxster & Cayman (Streather)
Porsche 986 Boxster (Streather)
Porsche 987 Boxster and Cayman 1st generation (2005-2009) (Streather)
Porsche 987 Boxster and Cayman 2nd generation (2009-2012) (Streather)
Range Rover – First Generation models 1970 to 1996 (Taylor)
Range Rover – Second Generation 1994-2001 (Taylor)
Range Rover – Third Generation L322 (2002-2012) (Taylor)
Reliant Scimitar GTE (Payne)
Rolls-Royce Silver Shadow & Bentley T-Series (Bobbitt)
Rover 2000, 2200 & 3500 (Marrocco)
Royal Enfield Bullet (Henshaw)
Subaru Impreza (Hobbs)
Sunbeam Alpine (Barker)
Triumph 350 & 500 Twins (Henshaw)
Triumph Bonneville (Henshaw)
Triumph Herald & Vitesse (Ayre)
Triumph Spitfire and GT6 (Ayre)
Triumph Stag (Mort)
Triumph Thunderbird, Trophy & Tiger (Henshaw)
Triumph TR2 & TR3 - All models (including 3A & 3B) 1953 to 1962 (Conners)
Triumph TR4/4A & TR5/250 - All models 1961 to 1968 (Child & Battyll)
Triumph TR6 (Williams)
Triumph TR7 & TR8 (Williams)
Triumph Trident & BSA Rocket III (Rooke)
TVR Chimaera and Griffith (Kitchen)
TVR S-series (Kitchen)
Velocette 350 & 500 Singles 1946 to 1970 (Henshaw)
Vespa Scooters – Classic 2-stroke models 1960-2008 (Paxton)
Volkswagen Bus (Copping)
Volkswagen Transporter T4 (1990-2003) (Copping/Cservenka)
VW Golf GTI (Copping)
VW Beetle (Copping)
Volvo 700/900 Series (Beavis)
Volvo P1800/1800S, E & ES 1961 to 1973 (Murray)

# www.veloce.co.uk

First published in June 2022 by Veloce Publishing Limited, Veloce House, Parkway Farm Business Park, Middle Farm Way, Poundbury, Dorchester DT1 3AR, England. Tel +44 (0)1305 260068 / Fax 01305 250479 / e-mail info@veloce.co.uk / web www.veloce.co.uk or www.velocebooks.com.
ISBN: 978-1-787117-64-8; UPC: 6-36847-01764-4.

# Introduction

Morgan began producing four-wheeler cars in 1936, and by the late 1960s a flagship model was sought to build upon the success of the Plus 4. With access to the Buick/Rover V8, the Plus 8 was born in 1968, and remained in continuous production until 2004. It was reintroduced in 2012 based on the Aero 8 platform, finally finishing production in 2018 with the 50th anniversary edition.

The Morgan Plus 8 was built only as a two-seater. However, there was one exception: a factory-built four-seater produced for Eric White of Allon White & Son Ltd, on the understanding it was not to be sold in either Eric or Peter Morgan's lifetime.

The aim of this book is to give you a detailed background of the model, as it has changed over the decades. It covers basic considerations such as running costs and common faults that can occur, as well as being an in-depth guide on what to look for when assessing a potential purchase. Although there are some heavily modified examples out there, this book concentrates on enthusiast-owned and typically found examples.

Chapter 9's easy-to-use evaluation system provides a method of working out a car's overall condition by adding up the points relating to each area of the car being viewed. It will either confirm that the car you are viewing is 'the one' or will help you to identify potential areas of expenditure.

The last section gives you vital data on the different versions since 1968. A full list of options is not provided for each year as this would take up a whole separate book; however, the key facts that will help you determine a genuine example are included.

A Morgan Plus 8 ready for the open road.

The author has over 28 years experience of working in a Morgan main dealership, from being a mechanic to selling in excess of 100 Morgans per year, and hopes that this book will instil confidence in assessing and purchasing a Plus 8, confirm your choice of model, and set you on your way in your quintessentially British Morgan journey.

## Thanks

A number of people have kindly helped in collating information and photographs for this book, their assistance has been invaluable.

**A 1997 short door interior.**

Thanks to: Melvyn Rutter for collaborating dates and for some key photographs; Keith Jackson from Brands Hatch Morgan for additional date collaboration; Aston Workshops for the pictures of the Le Mans 62; Peter Gardner for pictures of the four-seater Plus 4; Morgan Motor Company for the use of its media centre; and my family for putting up with me writing another book.

*Original Morgan* by John Worrall and Liz Turner (ISBN 9780760316443) is an excellent reference guide to all the traditional models, and has been a great help.

A typical club event; these are always well attended.

# Contents

---

**The Essential Buyer's Guide™ currency**
At the time of publication a BG unit of currency "●" equals approximately
£1.00/US$1.25/Euro 1.19. Please adjust to suit current exchange rates
using Sterling as the base rate.

# 1 Is it the right car for you?

– marriage guidance

## Tall and short drivers

Whether you are 5ft or 6ft 3in tall you should be able to fit into and drive a Morgan. There are two considerations for the taller driver: if you are long in the body, you'll need to check that you clear the hood when it is up. If you have an inside leg measurement of 33in or under you will be fine, but taller drivers may prefer a 14in steering wheel for comfort and to give clearance when changing gears.

The classic lines of an early Plus 8.

## Controls

Other than a couple of rare exceptions, all factory Plus 8s come with manual gearboxes: these were four-speed until 1976, and five-speed from then on. Power steering has never been an option on a Plus 8 – the lightness of the car means it isn't required, even on those with the 16in wire wheel option. Most buyers are pleasantly surprised by the feel and feedback of the standard steering setup. Remote servo assisted brakes were fitted until 1981, and then became standard again in 1992.

A beautiful walnut dashboard with toggle switches and a push-button starter.

Luggage rack with sidescreen storage: ideal for a large case.

## Will it fit in your garage?

Bumpers, overriders and differences in wheel size can make slight differences in the dimensions of each individual vehicle, but for the purposes of this guide maximum sizes are cited.

The dimensions are: 13ft long by 4ft 9in wide (3980mm by 1447mm) for the very early cars, and up to 5ft 6in (1710 mm) in width for a late example on wire wheels.

The interior of a long door model, with an offset steering wheel for a taller driver.

No two Plus 8s are the same. This example has been set up for fast road use.

### Usability
The model has classic 1930s looks with modern running gear. Although they're not normally used every day, they are certainly up to the job, and are an ideal 'classic' where you can turn the key and just go. They have traditional looks with that wonderful V8 burble, what's not to like?

### Parts availability
You will find excellent parts availability, with most still available from the Morgan factory via the dealer network. There is also a great range of specialists providing upgrades and some of the more obscure/older items.

### Insurance
Even a newer example can be insured on a classic car policy. Most buyers pay between ●180-●400 a year on a limited mileage policy. Typically, a Plus 8 is only around ●50 more to insure than a 4/4. Agreed values can be arranged with various specialist companies, and are strongly recommended.

### Running costs
These are remarkably low for such a specialised car. Standard models will easily achieve high fuel economy with up to 30mpg being achievable. Low insurance costs and good reliability mean a Morgan does not hit the pocket like some other classic sports cars.

### Prices and investment potential
Morgans are well known for holding their value. You would usually expect some depreciation; however, keeping the car for longer means the depreciation will be

spread out over a longer period of time. The value may well increase over time, but treat this as a potential bonus, you can expect to get the bulk of the purchase price back on resale, if you keep the car in good condition. Joy of ownership, touring, and the Morgan lifestyle should be the reasons for purchase.

## Alternatives

There isn't really a direct alternative. Other classic sports cars from the 1950s and 1960s could be considered for the character, or perhaps modern mass-produced sports cars with the latest engines and running gear. The Plus 8 has the best of both worlds: it is nicely placed with old world charm and character, but with modern reliable running gear, so you don't have to be mechanically minded, and won't have to tinker like you would with an older car.

This 1976 interior has a turned instrument panel and Brooklands steering wheel.

# 2 Cost considerations
– affordable, or a money pit?

Servicing is recommended every 5000 miles or at 12-month intervals. Later handbooks say 10,000 miles or 12-month intervals, but most owners struggle to complete anywhere near this mileage in 12 months. The earlier cars (until the late 1970s) recommended 3000 mile service intervals.

The Morgan Plus 8 has always been fitted with the Land Rover/Buick V8, although engine capacity has changed over the years. They are all chain-driven.

## Servicing costs
Medium service/5000 miles  .. .. .. .. .. .. .. .. .. .. .. .. .. .. .. .. . ●x470
Full service/10,000 miles  .. .. .. .. .. .. .. .. .. .. .. .. .. .. .. .. . ●x683
Brake fluid change.. .. .. .. .. .. .. .. .. .. .. .. .. .. .. .. .. .. .. .. ●x50

## Mechanical parts
Brake pads and discs. .. .. .. .. .. .. .. .. .. .. .. .. .. .. .. .. .. . ●x234
Rear wheel cylinders pre 1992  .. .. .. .. .. .. .. .. .. .. .. .. .. .. ●x50
Rear wheel cylinders 1992 on. .. .. .. .. .. .. .. .. .. .. .. .. .. .. ●x97
Clutch master cylinder  .. .. .. .. .. .. .. .. .. .. .. .. .. .. .. .. . ●x126
Clutch slave cylinder .. .. .. .. .. .. .. .. .. .. .. .. .. .. .. .. .. . ●x106
Standard kingpin  .. .. .. .. .. .. .. .. .. .. .. .. .. .. .. .. .. .. . ●x44
Kingpin bush (two required per side) .. .. .. .. .. .. .. .. .. .. .. ●x19
Rear leaf spring .. .. .. .. .. .. .. .. .. .. .. .. .. .. .. .. .. .. .. ●x206
Front main spring .. .. .. .. .. .. .. .. .. .. .. .. .. .. .. .. .. .. . ●x31
Radiator refurbishment .. .. .. .. .. .. .. .. .. .. .. .. .. .. .. .. ●x216
Upgraded aluminium radiator.. .. .. .. .. .. .. .. .. .. .. .. .. .. . ●x696
Trackrod end.. .. .. .. .. .. .. .. .. .. .. .. .. .. .. .. .. .. .. .. .. ●x45
Steering rack gaiter  .. .. .. .. .. .. .. .. .. .. .. .. .. .. .. .. .. ●x83
Handbrake cable  .. .. .. .. .. .. .. .. .. .. .. .. .. .. .. .. .. .. .●x101

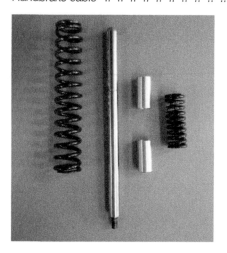

Typical parts required for a kingpin overhaul. Stub axle bushes will need reaming out once in place.

## Bodywork parts

| | |
|---|---:|
| Front wing 'Superform' aluminium | x1376 |
| Rear wing 'Superform' aluminium | x637 |
| Over rider (2003 on) | x260 |
| Stainless steel bumper (1998 on) with end caps | x637 |
| Windscreen glass up to 1998 | x228 |
| Heated windscreen assembly | x925 |
| Windscreen wiper blade | x13 |
| Door mirror | x58 |
| 16in chrome wire wheel | x487 |
| 15in alloy wheel | x206 |
| Original quality tyre 205/60 x15 | x90 |
| Galvanised chassis | x2010 |
| Valance (stainless steel) | x504 |

## Electrical items

| | |
|---|---:|
| Headlamp (pair) | x74 |
| Indicator lamp | x26 |
| Indicator stalk (to late 1997) | x84 |
| Sparkplug | x5 |
| Lambda/oxygen sensor | x120 |
| Ignition switch assembly | x136 |
| Starter motor (exchange) | x170 |

## Trim and restoration (examples)

| | |
|---|---:|
| New pvc hood | x935 |
| New mohair hood | x1125 |
| New pvc tonneau | x395 |
| Full interior retrim in leather | x4235 |
| New carpet set | x575 |
| Full bare metal repaint | x6500 |

# 3 Living with a Plus 8
– will you get along together?

There are a number of things to decide before buying a Morgan, and questions you should ask yourself: honest answers will help you choose the ideal model to suit your needs.

## What are you going to use the car for?

Local runs, car shows and country lanes, weekends away, regular commuting use, high-mileage touring holidays? If it is the latter, you may prefer a newer model. If you fancy the odd track day, or fast club runs – for instance, to Le Mans – maybe a previously tuned model may be better for you.

Standard seats with four-point harnesses for that sporty feel.

## Do you have children or need extra luggage capacity?

If yes, then you may prefer a four-seater, in which case look at a 4/4, Plus 4 or Roadster. However, consider the age of your children and whether they are interested in going out in a Morgan; children older than early teens and taller children may find the rear seats cramped. So, in reality, if the noise and low down torque of the Plus 8 is what you crave, go for it.

## What do you drive now?

Are you used to a larger engine, for example 3.0-litre or above? If so, the power

2004 uprated heated folding/reclining sports seats for extra comfort.

Bonnet louvres are individually hand pressed; the view is timeless, and is part of the Morgan's special character.

Perhaps you prefer a concours car? An immaculately detailed 1969 engine bay.

of the Plus 8 will feel similar. You may decide you would prefer something a little different and with a slightly lighter feel. In which case, it may be worth trying out a Plus 4 to compare the two. If your heart is set on a Plus 8, don't bother with a 4/4, as you're sure to think it underpowered and it will be a pointless exercise. Try to imagine yourself after three months of ownership – are you going to be happy with your choice?

### What mileage are you likely to cover?
Many owners cover only half of the mileage they expect to during a 12-month period, and 2500 miles per year is quite common. Work and life can take over, and, sadly, your Morgan gets left in the garage; lack of use is one of the main reasons for cars coming up for sale. Low mileage could save you money when buying insurance, however, by arranging a limited mileage policy.

### Which model age will suit you?
Morgans have evolved over the years, so a 1970 Plus 8 will feel very different to a 2000 example. The newer cars feel more modern and lighter to drive. If you're not sure which model age to go for, you'll need to try a few to see which one you fall in love with.

Every Morgan is different, there's a choice of 50,000 colours, over 30 leathers, and a long options list, so no two cars are ever the same. As they're handmade they all feel very slightly different, even compared to another example built on the same day. This is the soul of the car, and very few manufacturers or models have it. It's what you're buying into. You can't put your finger on what it is, but once you feel it you are hooked. So, despite its odd foibles, it will get under your skin, become part of the family, and could even be given a name.

Once you have the car, you'll be part of an extended family. The Morgan Sports

A 1991 Plus 8 in perfect touring weather.

Car Club (MSCC) is huge, with local area groups and regular events. Other owners, enthusiasts, and the public at large love the cars, and you will rarely hear of any vandalism, or attempted theft. You can leave your car almost anywhere and people will come up to talk to you and admire it. At some point in your ownership you should do a factory tour. You can see the build process and talk to the people who made your car. The experience is priceless.

If you want all the latest electronic driver aids, touch screens, climate control and top quality sound systems, then a Morgan Plus 8 probably isn't for you. If you want adventure, feel, and feedback through the steering, loads of character, the noise, and a heap of fun within the speed limits, then you will easily learn to live with the Plus 8.

Yes, the fly off handbrake takes a little getting used to. There is nowhere to put your clutch foot, you will learn to rest it on the pedal lightly (clutches rarely wear out, before you ask). Or you'll adjust the position of your foot so it is between the clutch and the brake pedals, after a while you will do it without thinking.

Getting in and out gracefully, especially with the hood up, takes a bit of practice. The interior is cosy, but the seats are comfortable, even the fixed backed ones. Expect the odd drip when it rains – it is a convertible.

Do you think you'll get along? If so, pin down the age range of the model and the budget you want to spend, and let the fun begin.

# 4 Relative values
– which model for you?

This chapter shows in percentage terms the relative value of each model produced since 1968. Using a Plus 8 1997-2001 as an example, a typical value of a 1977-1982 will be around 60% of a 1999 model. Every Morgan is different: value here assumes a car in good condition, with low mileage and a range of the common extras.

## Plus 8 3.5: Moss gearbox, 1968-1972
100%

A 1968 Plus 8 (Moss gearbox).

The 1972 Plus 8 four-seater. This is the only factory-built example.

## Plus 8 3.5: Rover four-speed gearbox, 1972-1976
80%

1976 Plus 8 3.5 (carburettor).

## Plus 8 3.5: five-speed gearbox, 14in wheels, 1977-1982
60%

1976-1981 Plus 8 3.5 (carburettor).

## Plus 8 3.5: five-speed, 15in alloy wheel, 1982-1987
70%

1983 Plus 8 3.5
(carburettor).

## Plus 8 3.5: five-speed injection, 1984-1990
70%

## Plus 8 3.9: 1990-1997
85%

1997 Plus 8 3.9.

## Plus 8 4.6: 1996-2001
85%
The first few cars made were short door models, the rest had long doors.

## Plus 8 3.9: long door, 1997-2001
100%

1999 Plus 8 long door.

## Plus 8 4.0: 2001-2004
110%

2000 Plus 8 4.6.

## Plus 8 Le Mans 62 edition, 2002
125%
Only 40 Plus 8s were produced, along with 40 4/4s.

2002 Plus 8 Le Mans 62.

## Plus 8 35th anniversary, 2003-2004
130%

2004 35th
anniversary
edition.

# 5 Before you view

– be well informed

To avoid a wasted journey, and the disappointment of finding that the car does not match your expectations, it will help if you're very clear about what questions you want to ask before you pick up the telephone. Some of these points might appear basic but when you're excited about the prospect of buying your dream classic, it's amazing how some of the most obvious things slip the mind ... Also check the current values of the chosen model in classic car magazines which give both a price guide and auction results.

## Where is the car?

Is it worth travelling a considerable distance to view? A locally advertised car, although it may not sound very interesting, can add to your knowledge for very little effort, so make a visit – it might even be in better condition than expected.

## Dealer or private sale?

Establish early on if the car is being sold by its owner or by a trader. A private owner should have all the history, so don't be afraid to ask detailed questions. A dealer may have more limited knowledge of a car's history, but should have some documentation. A dealer may offer a warranty/guarantee (ask for a printed copy) and finance.

## Cost of collection and delivery

A dealer may well be used to quoting for delivery by car transporter. A private owner may agree to meet you halfway, but only agree to this after you have seen the car at the vendor's address to validate the documents. Conversely, you could meet halfway and agree the sale but insist on meeting at the vendor's address for the handover.

## View – when and where?

It is always preferable to view at the vendor's home or business premises. In the case of a private sale, the car's documentation should tally with the vendor's name and address. Arrange to view only in daylight and avoid a wet day. Most cars look better in poor light or when wet.

## Reason for sale?

Do make this one of the first questions. Why is the car being sold and how long has it been with the current owner? How many previous owners?

## Steering conversions/specials

If a steering conversion has been done it may reduce the value and it may well be that other aspects of the car still reflect the specification for a foreign market.

## Condition (body/chassis/interior/mechanicals)

Ask for an honest appraisal of the car's condition. Ask specifically about some of the check items described in chapter 7.

## All original specification?

An original equipment car is invariably of higher value than a highly modified version.

## Matching data/legal ownership

Do VIN/chassis, engine numbers and licence plate match the official registration document? Is the owner's name and address recorded in the official registration documents? For those countries that require an annual test of roadworthiness, does the car have a document showing it complies? (An MOT certificate in the UK, which can be verified on 0300 123 9000 or www.gov.uk/check-mot-status.) If a smog/emissions certificate is mandatory, does the car have one? If required, does the car carry a current road fund licence/licence plate tag? Does the vendor own the car outright? Money might be owed to a finance company or bank: the car could even be stolen. Several organisations will supply the data on ownership, based on the car's licence plate number, for a fee. Such companies can often also tell you whether the car has been 'written-off' by an insurance company. In the UK these organisations can supply vehicle data:

| | | | |
|---|---|---|---|
| DVLA | 0844 453 0118 | HPI | 0113 222 2010 |
| AA | 0800 056 8040 | RAC | 0330 159 0364 |

Other countries will have similar organisations.

## Unleaded fuel?

All Plus 8s are able to run on unleaded fuel, however customers report older examples run a lot better on 98 RON super unleaded rather than the 95 RON. With the introduction of E10 fuel, it is recommended to run the cars on the E5 super unleaded. The odd tank of E10, if E5 isn't available will not cause immediate damage to hoses and carburettor parts. A number of lead replacement additives contain ethanol neutralisers, so having a bottle handy is a good idea.

## Insurance

Check with your existing insurer before setting out, your current policy might not cover you to drive the car if you do purchase it.

## How you can pay

A cheque/check will take several days to clear and the seller may prefer to sell to a cash buyer. A banker's draft is safer than a cheque, but you'll need to organise this with your bank and may also need time for it to clear. A direct bank transfer is usually the quickest and easiest method.

## Buying at auction?

If the intention is to buy at auction see chapter 10 for further advice.

## Professional vehicle check (mechanical examination)

There are marque/model specialists who will undertake professional examination of a vehicle on your behalf. Owners' clubs will be able to put you in touch with such specialists. Other organisations that will carry out a general professional check in the UK:

| | |
|---|---|
| AA | 0800 056 8040 / www.theaa.com/vehicle-inspection (motoring organisation with vehicle inspectors) |
| RAC | 0330 159 0720 / www.rac.co.uk/buying-a-car/vehicle-inspections; (motoring organisation with vehicle inspectors) |

Other countries will have similar organisations.

# 6 Inspection equipment

– these items will really help

Go prepared, remember the list of questions you probably left on the coffee table and take the following items:

**This book**
**Reading glasses (if you need them for close work)**
**Magnet (fridge magnet is ideal)**
**Torch (flashlight or mobile phone light)**
**Probe (a small screwdriver)**
**Overalls and a cushion/pillow**
**Mirror on a stick**
**Digital camera**
**A friend, preferably a knowledgeable enthusiast**

**This book**
This book is designed to be your guide, so take it along and use the check boxes in chapter 9 to help you assess each area of the car you're interested in. Don't be afraid to let the seller see you using it.

**Reading glasses (If you need them for close work)**
For checking paperwork and close inspections; you would be amazed how many people forget to take them.

## Magnet (fridge magnet is ideal)
Wrap the magnet in a thin soft cloth and gain permission before using it on the body panels. Most later cars will have aluminium panels, which magnets will not stick to. Wings could be made of steel or aluminium up until 1998, then aluminium only from 1998. Aftermarket fibreglass wings are available and may have been fitted during accident repairs or restoration. Some filler around the headlamps on both types of wings is to be expected. At least you will know what type of panels are fitted.

## Torch (flashlight or mobile phone light)
Ideal to check those dark areas of the engine bay, underside and inside the car. Ensure it has fresh batteries or is fully charged.

## Probe (a small screwdriver)
Use finger pressure to check and only use the probe if something needs further examination. Check with the vendor first before using it and explain why you wish to check a certain area.

## Overalls and a cushion/pillow
You will get dirty when you are checking the underside and mechanical parts. Wear disposable gloves or ensure you wash your hands before touching any of the interior, paintwork or weather equipment. Use the cushion to kneel on when visually checking in the footwells and underside.

## Mirror on a stick
Handy to view those in 'hard to see' areas particularly when combined with using a torch.

## Digital camera (or smartphone)
You may find it useful to take pictures for reference, or if you want to seek a second opinion on an area of concern.

# 7 Fifteen minute evaluation
– walk away or stay?

Be objective, it's easy to let your heart rule your head when viewing. Remember 'All that glitters is not gold.' Despite the value of the Plus 8, you are looking at a used car, which may be older than it appears, and unlikely to be in an as-new condition.

## Exterior

Starting at one corner walk around the car, and record any noticeable damage to the bodywork, for example, dents, stone chips, paint condition and corrosion, particularly on the wing edges. Being handmade, tolerances can vary but they should be consistent. Do the bonnets and doors fit well? Is there a gap on the bonnet centre strip to the brass hinge ends? If so, this indicates that the cowl may have been removed at some point. Doors rubbing at the bottom of the screen deck or the elbow panel is common, particularly on older cars.

Open the bonnets (to open release the rear catch first and then the front; to close do the front catch first, then the rear – you'll learn the technique). Bonnet straps shouldn't have to hold down the bonnets, they are for decoration only. Wings should fit neatly up to the bulkhead, with neat slotted screws, not misplaced large bolts. Bonnets should not have rubbed on the tops of the wings: if they have you are looking at a fair amount of time and expense to put this right, or it can be a sign of something more sinister, such as a poorly executed rebuild.

There should be a join between the screen deck and the elbow panel about halfway along the door: this join should not be filled in. The elbow panels can crack slightly further back; this could be just a stress crack from the panel fittings, due to time and use, or could be a sign of deterioration of the wood frame. Make a note to check in more detail if any cracks are found.

The bonnet centre strip hinge gap highlights if the cowl and bonnets have been removed. This one needs realigning, and the bonnet paint also shows micro blistering.

The panel join under the door, between the screen deck and elbow panel, is clearly shown with this new elbow panel.

Until 1972, the cars had a flat rear panel with a strip running down each side; from 1972 the strips disappeared and the rear panel wrapped around the sides. Check the lower corners of the rear panel for impact marks. If bumpers are fitted, are they straight? Bumpers can easily be nudged, causing the sweep and mounting bolt to flex on impact – thus puncturing the rear panel – and then spring back into the original position. The panel can be repaired, though a lot of owners don't spot this kind of damage.

Stand back and check that the car is sitting level. View from different angles to see if the car lists to one side. Rear springs can sag and kingpins can stick, causing the car to be lower on one corner.

Check the windscreen for damage (heated screens from 1998 are expensive to replace). Look out for delamination from the lower corners, and cracks from the mounting screws on the side of the screen, which could be caused by a shrunken hood.

## Wheels and tyres

Tyres are date stamped, and, even if there is good tread depth, check for age-related cracks, particularly on Pirelli tyres. If the tyres are over ten years old they will definitely need to be changed, regardless of condition.

Morgan's own rough-cast five-stud Magnesium alloy 15in wheels were fitted 1968-1976. These had a 5.5in rim width, changing to 6.5in rims in 1971, and were fitted with Dunlop SP 185 R 15 tyres.

Milrace 14in alloy wheels with a 6in rim width were fitted between 1977 and early 1982. These were normally paired with

Stainless wire wheels are a different colour compared to chrome, with a hint of yellow. Look at the wheel nut on this stainless example.

195 R 15 tyres, or occasionally 205 R 15 tyres from 1980. The eight-slotted alloy wheel area is normally silver, but 19 Sports lightweight examples had this area painted black, with the rest of the rim and slots outlined in silver.

From 1982, Morgan commissioned its own 15in 6.5in rim alloy wheel, which has been used continuously since that date. It was also used until 2020 on Roadsters and later Plus 4s as an option. Looking similar to the original 1968 wheel, it has the words 'Morgan Motor Company Ltd' in the casting. Occasionally, during the early years of production, the outside edge of the rim could be diamond cut for a more polished finish. These wheels were fitted with 205/60 R 15 tyres, with Pirelli, Avon and Uniroyal being the standard fit during the 1980s and 1990s.

16in chrome wire wheels with a 7in rim width became a cost option in 1993. These wheels have stainless steel spokes with chrome rims, and a tyre size of 205/55 R 16.

From 2003, stainless wire wheels were offered with the same tyre size. The Le Mans 62 edition had a 16in stainless wheel with a 6in rim. The chrome wheels can rust quite badly over time, or you may find the chrome has been over-polished, and the base plating shows through.

Note: the wings on wire-wheeled cars are wider than on those with alloys, to accommodate the offset of the wheels. This makes the cost to convert from alloys to wire wheels prohibitive. Aftermarket wheels are available that don't require the wings to be changed, but to a trained eye do not look factory-fitted.

From 1995-2001 a 16in centre-lock alloy wheel was an option. If these are fitted you can do a direct swap to the 16in factory wire wheels. These centre-lock wheels are rarely seen, but we've found the inside bead rims can corrode and cause slow punctures.

## Underside and bulkhead

Examine the underside, bulkhead and valances (inner wings) next. The bulkhead and valances were factory undersealed until 1986, this finish can be more durable than the later versions. On cars produced between 1986-1998 these parts were powder coated and undersealed, a practice that coincided with 'wings off' paintwork becoming officially standard. The powder coated panels can deteriorate quite quickly. If the bulkhead powder coating is in good original order it is an indicator of how the car has been kept. It is also very common for the bulkheads on 1986-1998 cars to have been repainted or treated with Hammerite. From 1998 the bulkhead and valances became stainless, and the bulkheads are often changed to stainless steel versions during restoration.

On the driver's side, where the steering shaft is mounted and goes through the

An extremely rusty bulkhead, with the heater box removed. This one is beyond repair.

Stainless bulkheads were introduced in 1998, and can now be fitted to earlier cars during restoration or accident repair.

valance, the panel is double skinned. The panel can corrode in this area, along the lower section and at the rear by the bulkhead. The valances can be changed with the front wing in situ, but you'll need to allow for eight to ten hours labour per side.

The bulkhead can rot where the valances bolt on, where it mounts into the chassis, and where the toolbox is mounted on the earlier cars, but can be repaired if the top of the bulkhead is in good order.

## Chassis

A galvanised chassis has been an option since 1989, and became standard in 1998. Check an early steel chassis for rust in the following places: under the triangle plates by the front crossmembers; along the chassis rails where the floorboards are mounted; lever arm rear shock absorber mountings; and the rear crossmember. Visually check all the crossmembers. Galvanised chassis can crack, particularly in the engine bay area, so do not assume that because it's galvanised it will be fine. Don't be put off by a car with a non-galvanised chassis, if the chassis is in good condition it will last for years. Even 40-year-old cars can still have an excellent original chassis.

You can see the bulk of the chassis from inside the engine bay and from the underside of the car. Check the chassis number is present: on earlier cars it's stamped on the crossmember behind the driver's seat, and on cars from 1998 it's on the crossmember in front of the driver's seat. The later cars will have a 17-digit chassis number.

Check the chassis for damage, and for ripples along the sides and flat sections. Although the Plus 8 is of a relatively simple ladder-type construction, there is a limit to what can be straightened. Frontal damage impact force will travel down the length of the car, and may cause ripples in the chassis rails near to the axle. Check this carefully if the car has been classified as an insurance total loss, and been rebuilt.

## Wood frame

Morgan cars have never had a wooden chassis. The wooden body frame is mounted onto a metal chassis. The body frame is constructed of ash, then panelled in steel or aluminium. The frames have been treated with Cuprinol since 1986 as standard; some earlier cars are known to have been treated from 1984. It is rare to have wood issues on the later cars. However, you still need to check the frame. Earlier frames up to 1972 were of a thinner construction, and this is noticeable on the thickness of the hinge post.

Open the doors and check for play: a little play in the door hinges is normal, particularly on the driver's side. Also check that the hinge post doesn't move at the bottom. Check the tacks on the threshold strips: if any are missing or coming adrift this could be a sign that the rocker has gone soft. You can check the rocker by feeling (carefully) with your finger and thumb along the inside, just under the draught excluder. Feel the edge of the wood along the top and side, working from front to back. The rear sections can rot, in which case you'll find the edge suddenly disappears. Using only finger pressure, you won't do any damage to the interior trim. With the door still open, and with light pressure, hold the top of the elbow rail and see if there is any play or movement in the bottom joint. Definitely check this area if there is a split starting to form in the elbow panel.

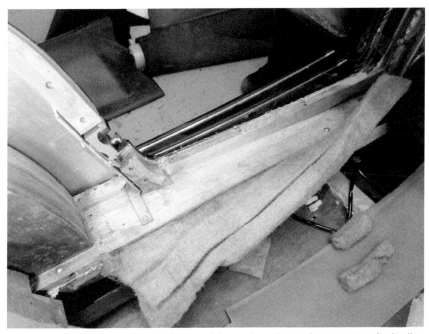

Sillboard and rocker sections of the wood frame: key pieces that can rot quite badly.

Check under the front wing where it mounts on the sill board, light pressure can be applied to check the wood condition.

Check inside the rear wheelarches, particularly in the corners, and the rear

Plastic rear lamp bezels were fitted from 1971; some were chrome plated (as seen here) from the mid-1970s until the early 1980s. Stainless replacements are now available.

frame where the back panel mounts onto it. The rear frame is commonly referred to as the 'rear goal post,' and the joints can deteriorate.

If the Plus 8 has bumpers – most do – check the number plate panel. If it is loose, check that the mounting screws are secure, and that the wood behind the panel is sound.

## Interior

Vinyl, also known as Ambla, was standard fitment, with leather being a cost option. The original leather ranges were the Connolly HB pack or the Autolux ranges. It is now extremely difficult to obtain HB-style leathers with the antique looking grain, due to current tanning techniques. Muirhead leathers were used from 2002.

Ambla is very hard-wearing, but it is common for the material to tear or split on the seats due to deterioration of the stitching.

Check the leather condition. If it's saggy on the sill boards, double check the wood, as the padding may have become soaked, causing wet rot. Water staining of the leather on the sills is quite common on cars that have been used in all weathers. Water that gets in accumulates on the sills, especially if the sidescreens have not been properly tucked into the hood.

Wear on the driver's seat edge and on the elbow panel edge is to be expected. Elbow rail protectors can be purchased to improve this area. Bright-coloured leathers show more wear than darker shades, even on very low mileage cars.

The driver's seat base webbing can collapse. This may be the case if the seat cushion looks very flat, or you feel as if you are sitting in the frame rather than on the seat. Headrests were optional until 1998. Two-prong fittings were used until 1982; single-prong headrests have been used since.

Walnut dashboards have been an optional extra from 1986, but they can bleach and crack if exposed to strong sunlight. Rubber matting was fitted in the earlier cars, changing to carpet in 1974. Carpets can also bleach in the sun, and become bald in places due to wear, damp or moth damage, particularly under the seats.

The rear board behind the seats can be lifted out; this is a great way of

Standard leather seats on a 1985 example. Light leathers can show more wear than darker colours.

looking at the rear suspension or to see if the tool tray is intact (as fitted on post-2003 cars).

### Weather equipment

The earlier studded windscreen hoods take a bit of practice to put up. Once you have mastered the technique, though, it will take approximately two minutes. Later hoods, introduced in 2003, are easier to fit, and can be lowered more quickly. You can also release the rear of the later hood to access the luggage area.

Up to mid-2003, Plus 8s were supplied with a black vinyl studded type roof, outer sidescreens, and a tonneau. Coloured PVC/vinyl and mohair (from the mid 1980s) were cost options. Half tonneaus and hood frame covers have also become popular options over the last couple of decades.

From late 2003 the Plus 8 was fitted with Morgan's new easier-fitting '20-second'/'easy-up' hood in black vinyl, and with sidescreens. Options included a tonneau cover, coloured PVC and mohair.

On the later cars weather equipment was available in either coloured PVC or mohair packs, in addition to the hood itself, with the choice being either a hood frame cover and sidescreen bag, or a tonneau and sidescreen bag.

Customers quite often have additional weather equipment made from a mix of the available materials, for example a PVC hood with a mohair hood frame cover. The main point is that there should be weather equipment with the car. If it is there, check that it all fits, and has all its fixings.

The final factory hood design: the '20-second' easy-fit hood. Similar aftermarket designs are available.

There is a technique for putting the hood up (both styles), and the vendor should know how to do this (if not, there are a number of videos available online). Aftermarket easier fitting hoods are available for the earlier style models, and may be desirable on a used car.

Hood condition is important. Hoods are not off-the-shelf items, but are made to fit the individual car. There are pros and cons on both types of material: PVC/vinyl can shrink with age, discolour (this is particularly noticeable with those in the stone colour), and become stiff in cold weather. However, it is easier to clean than mohair and cheaper to replace. Mohair can get baggy, blister with age, fade, and show wear marks on the later easy-fit style hoods, due to how the hood is folded. Mohair has a more attractive appearance, though, which is why it is often chosen. Tonneau zips can break, so check that these are intact and operational.

## Mechanicals and electrics

Check the following items under the bonnet: fluid levels, particularly the clutch fluid level, hose condition, wiring condition, and heater foams. Check inside the toolbox, if fitted, to ensure all items are present. Check all for signs of rodent damage or rust. From the mid 1980s to the early 1990s a vacuum-formed heater foam was fitted on the heater box, these foams disintegrate with age and have been unavailable for at least 20 years. If it is in good condition it can indicate that the car has had a sheltered life, but the foams are usually removed if they have deteriorated too badly.

## Start the car

Does the engine crank over okay on the starter motor? Are there any strange noises, particularly from the engine, gearbox/clutch area or exhaust? Are there leaks from the cooling system or engine? With the engine running, look underneath to see if there are fluids dripping down anywhere. While the car is warming up, check the electrics work.

The newer the car, the less chance there is of oil leaks or oil misting on engine surfaces. Heavy oxidisation of the engine bay components can indicate the car has spent a lot of time outside or been used in all weathers.

Rover V8 engines can leak from the rocker cover gaskets, sump gaskets, rear main oil seals and front crankshaft seals. Expect the engine to be slightly wet as they are rarely oil-tight, but it shouldn't be excessive. Check for lumpy running and misfires, and for strange noises from the drivebelt area.

By now you should have a feel for the overall condition of the car, and whether to continue your inspection or to make your excuses and leave.

If all's good so far, then it's time for the more detailed inspection (using the scoring system in chapter 9), paying extra attention to the areas where you have noted concerns.

# 8 Key points
– where to look for problems

## Weather equipment

Check that all weather equipment is present and that it fits. Ideally, replacements are bespoke to ensure a good fit. Does the tonneau zip close fully when the tonneau is fitted? If the headrests are fitted, wiggle them and lift out to check the condition of the seat material.

The standard studded hood fitted from 1968-2002. The hoods changed from three bars to two from late 2002, until the easy-fit hood was launched.

## Radiators and cooling

Morgan radiators, whether made of brass or aluminium, can leak. This is generally around the top and bottom necks or from the main core. Aftermarket aluminium radiators with a larger capacity core are popular and rarely leak, but should still be checked. Check for overheating and that the coolant fan works. This is critical on a Plus 8.

Leaking radiators are a common issue. Aluminium replacements are the usual upgrade.

## Clutch cylinders
Check the fluid level, as cylinder leaks are common. In extreme cases you can lose clutch pedal pressure when driving.

## Electrical problems
Older cars can suffer with faulty gauges, poor earths on lights, and corroded terminals. Ensure the electronic ignition and fuel-injection systems work properly on later cars, as they can give occasional problems.

## Wood frame
Check the following: movement in door hinge posts, sill boards, missing or loose threshold strip tacks. Cracked elbow panels are a possible sign of a weak lower joint.

## Interior condition
Leather may be worn, particularly on the seats, and can shrink on the sill board areas. Seat base webbing can collapse. Carpets fade.

This 1996 Plus 8 interior has standard fixed back seats with the headrests removed, along with a chrome mirror, walnut dashboard and Moto-Lita steering wheel.

## Wings and general paint condition
Wings can corrode around the edges: look for bubbling and evidence of repair. Check for evidence of accident repair or poorly executed paint repairs.

Aluminium wing showing corrosion.

A stripped down chassis showing fuel tank mounting boards and telescopic rear shock absorber bar.

## Valance condition

Valances pre-1998 can corrode, sometimes badly. Carefully check the one on the driver's side, as this is a structural item for the UK MOT (vehicle safety check).

Left: Chassis corrosion in front footwell. Note the bulkhead lower mounting location.
Right: An extremely corroded driver's side valance.

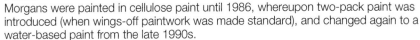

# 9 Serious evaluation
## – 60 minutes for years of enjoyment

Score each section using the boxes as follows:
4 = Excellent; 3 = good; 2 = average; 1 = poor. The totting up procedure is detailed at the end of the chapter. Be realistic in your marking!

## Paint

Morgans were painted in cellulose paint until 1986, whereupon two-pack paint was introduced (when wings-off paintwork was made standard), and changed again to a water-based paint from the late 1990s.

'Wings-on' paintwork can be identified by the wing beading being painted over in the body colour, while on 'wings-off' paintwork the beading is unpainted.

Plus 8s don't have the paint code on the chassis plate. Unless there's a reference to it in the service history, the only record of original colour will be on the sales invoice or in the Morgan factory records.

Check the quality of the paintwork on each panel. Is the finish even? Does the colour match the surrounding panels? Due to the angles and position of adjacent panels they can

Cars were painted with the wings on until 1986. The paint on the beading is prone to cracking.

An early torpedo sidelight, fitted until 1971.

This wing shows the later sidelight, with paintwork cracks around the light, headlamp pod, and part-way down the wing.

37

appear to be different colours, but you're basically checking for consistency. Ask the seller if any panels have been repainted; it's quite common for paintwork to have been carried out, even after a few years. Look out for localised repairs on the wings (they are expensive to paint due to the amount of work required for a good finish). You can usually see an edge like a tideline on localised repairs (see chapter 14 Paint problems).

## Body tub panels and rear wings    ④ ③ ② ①

Now examine the body tub in more detail, particularly on older cars. Panel fit should be good. Start at the front on one side and make your way around the car. Door handles were an option until 1997, whereupon they became a standard fitment, and not having them became a chargeable option. Open the door and check for

Even with an aluminium panelled car the screen deck and cowl were steel on all models until 2002. Note the difference in colour of the panels, and the various panel join lines.

rubbing of the inner skin against the lower screen deck section and on the elbow panel: the top rear corner of the door can rub into the elbow panel causing a little worn triangle. The bodies do flex, so some wear will occur with use. Is this wear consistent with the mileage and age of the car?

Aluminium body tubs were an option for decades before becoming standard in 1998, so the earlier cars may therefore have steel door skins; check with a magnet if you're unsure. The outer door skins can bubble towards the bottom. If the sidescreens are installed, remove them and check the paintwork around the mounting bracket; paintwork can bubble around the screw holes. Screen decks were also made of steel until 2002. Make sure the door hinge beading strip is in place – this was soldered on cars up to 2002, and can be awkward to refit during restoration.

Examine the lower section of the screen deck and elbow panel where it joins the wing beading; rust can bubble up along this area. Have a close look at the wing and around the wing tread areas for bubbling and localised repairs.

Continue over the elbow panel, towards the rear where it joins the back panel. Look carefully for paint repairs at the top of the panels and for overspray on the interior trim edges. Examine the rear panel, and, if bumpers are fitted, recheck for impact damage; it's easy to miss. Check the number plate mounting panel for corrosion around the edges, and that it's not loose. Wing beading fit should be tight between the panels.

Examine the rear wings: look at each one at the 12 o'clock position and note how many fingers you can get between the wing edge and outer edge of the tyre; the gap should be consistent on both sides of the car. Check the wing edges for corrosion, chips on the front face, and dents where people have leant on them when getting in and out. Look out for cracked paint, and for bulges when viewed from the rear to the front of the car. It is very common for the rear wings to be nudged on the rear corners, the wing then bows out and can crack the paint on the 10mm bead edge at the top of the wing edge between the 10 and 11 o'clock positions when viewed square on at this point. A minor kink can be pulled back straight, more serious damage may need the wing to be professionally reshaped and repainted. Also look at the bottom of the rear wing beading for corrosion and for scrape damage.

Stand back from the car and check the ride height by looking at the gap from the top of each rear tyre to the bottom of the wing at the 12 o'clock position. Up to an inch (25mm) difference is within manufacturer tolerances, but anything more may indicate suspension issues.

### Front wings, bonnets and cowl

Examine the front wings carefully: check panel fit, paint finish and for corrosion. Pre-1998 wings are non-superform, they are constructed in five sections, so can corrode part way down the vertical side of the wing as well as around the edges.

Cutting-in of the wings is an important area to check.

Left: Early chrome door locks as fitted until 1971. Right: Lucas L672 rear lamps and glass lens indicators were standard until 1971, changing to the round lamps, as per this 1972 example.

All pre-1998 wings have a ¾in (19mm) inner lip running down most of the length of the wing, and stays are attached to this area. Post-1998 cars don't have the lip, and the wing support stay is bonded on.

The 10mm bead edge running around the base of the wing is also bonded onto these later cars, and some of the early wings from this time can suffer paint bubbling due to a reaction with the bonding agent. It should also be noted that some wings produced from 1988-1990 had a wider bead edge; approximately 12mm deep rather than the usual 10mm.

Aluminium wings up to 1998 have a steel rod fitted around the inside – the aluminium is wrapped around it at the edge. Water ingress can be a problem in this area, causing an electrolytic reaction that corrodes the wing edge and exposes the rod. This is costly to put right; a new wing may be an easier and cheaper solution. Steel wings can also corrode in the same place, though it's easier to carry out weld repairs.

### Other points to note

The headlamp mounting position varies depending on age: ensure the gaps to the cowl and the outer section of the front wing are consistent on both sides. Paint can crack around the headlamps. There's less filler applied to the superform wings reducing the risk of cracking. Cars with sidelights mounted on the wings have a bracket underneath with a thin rubber pad (torpedo lamps were fitted until 1972, then larger lamps were fitted as standard until the end of production). The sidelight bolt hole can corrode and the bracket may eventually wear a hole in the wing. This can be repaired by welding in a new section.

The bonnets and cowl should fit well. There should be an even gap around the screen deck area, with no noticeable gap between the chrome strip and bonnet brass ends.

Check the cowl for impact damage from behind: it could have been dented if the radiator was removed in the past. Look to see if the heater platform has rubbed on the inner bonnet surfaces. Air filter trunking can also rub on the inner faces of the bonnet.

The gap between the bonnet and the top of the wing should be consistent side-to-side, though the gap is larger on later cars. Bonnet tape on all cars from 1986

The bulkhead can be removed with the body in situ.

should not be painted, but be natural coloured with a light coating of grease. Check the paintwork around the bonnet louvres, particularly on 1990s models, as the paint can flake off due to poor etch priming.

## Chassis, bulkhead and valances

Although covered in section 7, go over these again in more detail (especially pre-1990 cars) looking for cracks, corrosion, and possible accident damage along the chassis rails. Examine the valances and bulkhead carefully, especially on pre-

stainless steel cars. If a car is pre-1998 and has stainless valances, they may have already been changed due to corrosion or possible accident damage. Fittings should be consistent on both sides of the car. Lots of fresh bolts or underseal on one side indicates repairs: investigate in more detail.

Valances can be replaced with the front wing in place.

A metal ladder frame chassis: this is a post-1994 car, as the crossmember behind the driver's seat is inverted to allow the seat to slide further back.

## Brightwork

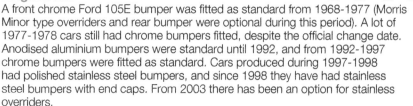

A front chrome Ford 105E bumper was fitted as standard from 1968-1977 (Morris Minor type overriders and rear bumper were optional during this period). A lot of 1977-1978 cars still had chrome bumpers fitted, despite the official change date. Anodised aluminium bumpers were standard until 1992, and from 1992-1997 chrome bumpers were fitted as standard. Cars produced during 1997-1998 had polished stainless steel bumpers, and since 1998 they have had stainless steel bumpers with end caps. From 2003 there has been an option for stainless overriders.

Check the bumpers for damage alignment and condition. Chrome bumpers can corrode and pit quite badly, and those produced since 1992 discolour in the area of the exhaust. If overriders are present, look out for impact damage.

Examine the inner and outer headlamp rims, number plate lamp covers and the door mirror bases and stems. They can all pit and corrode badly. The cost to replace is not excessive, but a good coat of wax polish will help protect them. Heavy use of chrome cleaners will remove the chrome over time, and pre-2002 front grilles are particularly susceptible to showing the base coating. Post-2002 grilles are stainless. Make sure the grille slats are attached at the top.

There were several types of door mirror fitted over time, the smaller ones with the nut to adjust the height have been obsolete for years. The mirror heads are usually stainless, but the bases and stems are not. Aftermarket items are available, including fully stainless with different mirror heads. Passenger mirrors were fitted as standard from 1998. Sidelights on the wings may not be wired up post-1998 as the real sidelight was mounted in the headlamp unit from that point to meet regulations. Check any remaining chromework including door handles and aerials. Luggage racks were originally painted grey, then chrome, before being manufactured in stainless steel; most racks are now of the stainless steel type.

Left: Original chrome bumper design.

Centre: Anodised aluminium bumper; the Marchal spot lamps were fitted from 1982-1985.

Bottom: The stainless bumper similar to the chrome bumper introduced in 1992.

Windscreens can crack, suffer stone chips, and delaminate. All three issues can be seen here.

## Wood frame
Double-check your initial findings regarding hinge post movement, loose tacks in the door threshold strips, and movement in the body joints. Post-1986 wood frames are treated and give little trouble, but you should still check.

## Windscreen
Studded windscreens were fitted until 2003; later windscreens are stud free, although there is an option for a studded screen. Heated windscreens have been fitted as standard from 1998. It is difficult to check the operation, though, so you may need to ask the vendor. Windscreen glasses de-laminate with age – identified by a 'milky' edge around the outside of the glass, usually beginning around the lower front corners. Check for wiper blade damage and stone chips, particularly around the interior mirror area, as they are easy to miss here. Check the glass fits the frame. Gaps at the bottom on repaired screens are not uncommon, and are usually hidden with sealant. New windscreen glass is available or can be cut for the non-heated screens. For heated windscreens it's usual practice to change the whole windscreen: Morgan changed manufacturers at some point, and the shape of the glass can vary in relation to the frame. This is only evident when stripping down the assembly. It is very expensive to replace them, so make sure you have adequate windscreen cover on your insurance. Cracks in the glass can be caused by over-tight hoods, or when owners pull on the frames to get in and out of the car. The cracks usually start from the mounting screws (three per side).

Check the chromework around the screen and the mounting pillars for corrosion. Wind deflectors may have been fitted to the side of the windscreen; if the screws are too long, cracks can occur. When sidescreens are fitted it's easy to trap the deflectors when closing the door, thus cracked or broken deflectors are common. Glass deflectors are available and are mounted slightly differently.

## Weather equipment

Although you would have already checked that the weather equipment fits, as mentioned in section 7, recheck the condition of each piece now. Look for fittings coming adrift, particularly the 'lift a dot' fasteners and turn-button plates on pre-2004 hoods and tonneaus. The hood stitching can pull apart at the front on the studded windscreen design, and it's not easy to repair without using a patch. The side of the hood towards the rear of the sidescreen area can split on both styles, due to stretching when owners get in and out.

The turn buttons on the body can break off and the binding around the rear of the hood can also split.

The fully removable hoods on the earlier cars can shrink if left folded or stored away. If the hood has not been put on for a long time, ensure that it still fits. Aftermarket swivel pins assist with the fitting of the hood, especially if it's a tight one.

Aftermarket easy-fit hood with sidescreen in place.

For later cars, check the side Tenax fastener on the elbow panel is intact and that it fits when the hood is up. It's common for hoods to be stored during the winter – this is recommended – but owners often forget to fit the Tenax, so the hood can shrink in this area. The header rail seal should be in place and not creased. Header rail side mount brackets can shear off at their weld point – usually due to over-tightening of the cant rail to stop rattles. Check the rear frame locks in position and that the frame is not broken.

Le Mans 62 editions were supplied with a cream hard top.

If the car has a roll bar fitted, check to see if the tonneau has been modified to accommodate it. Roll bars are normally added post production, and an owner may not have bothered altering it.

Check the sidescreen condition and that the lower pouch screws are there, as they can fall out, and also that the sidescreen rubbers are in good condition.

## Interior trim

Examine in more detail any areas of concern noted in your 15-minute inspection. Has the interior has been re-dyed? If so, the colour of the leather may look painted on rather than its original finish. The odd areas that have been treated for scuffs and wear can be expected on older examples, but do not assume you will be able to match worn areas easily. Lighter interiors might look more worn than darker interiors, although they can look roomier with the hood up. Stone and biscuit leather, although fairly light, are quite practical colours as they don't show dust and dirt as easily as darker colours. Water stains or drips on the gearbox cover are common, often due to the wiper spindle bezel gaskets not sealing – gently tightening the bezel nut can cure this issue.

Leather-optioned cars up to 1982 can have a mix of leather and vinyl. This is particularly noticeable on cars with a stone interior from the mid 1970s onward. You will probably find that a lot of older cars have been partly or fully retrimmed by now.

## Seat condition and operation

Plus 8s were originally fitted with fixed-back seats, with optional folding reclining Restall seats (as per the four-seater models from 1975). These Restall seats had the

Very early interior trimmed in ambla/vinyl. There is no crash padding on the top of the dashboard, but it has textured seat inserts.

provision for a two-prong headrest in each seat; however they were rarely supplied, and have become a popular aftermarket addition.

The two-seater bucket seats from 1975 also had the fittings in the seat frame for headrests, but these were often trimmed over during production, with the chrome locating fixings appearing later.

Owners have been known to change the seats to racing- or barrel-style bucket seats. Don't be put off if this is the case, but check that you find them comfortable.

In 1982, fixed seatbacks with single pin headrest holes were introduced. The headrests remained optional until 1998. The folding reclining seat has a flat seatback, and is commonly referred to as a tombstone seat. Sports seats were introduced as an option in 1995, these had a fixed back with added side support and full seat tilt mechanism to enable you to access the rear storage area. The tilt mechanism disappeared a few years later. The later reclining sports seats have more side support and were an option from 2003. Seats are normally mounted on wooden blocks, depending on when the car was built; if fitted, and if you need to raise the seat you can add in taller blocks!

Seat base webbing sometimes collapses along the rubber membrane (you can lift the seat cushion on some seats to check this membrane). Seats with side supports tend to wear on the raised areas. Check the piping for wear, and the back of the seats for luggage damage.

## Seatbelts and door locks
Examine the seatbelts for frays, mould and operation. Inertia seatbelts were not

Optional folding reclining seats: these had twin prong headrest holes from 1976-1982, and single prong headrests from 1982.

Fixed back sports seats: in earlier models the whole seat frame tilted forward for access, but this feature was dropped.

standard until 1986, but if they are fitted ensure the belts retract correctly. The passenger seatbelt from 1998 has a secondary ratchet (the pitch changes as you draw out the belt) that locks to allow a child seat to be installed. Chunks out of the belt webbing edge are surprisingly common, and are usually caused when the belt hasn't retracted properly and gets trapped in the door lock as someone gets out of the car. The belts are sometimes slow to retract, either due to seat position or, in the later cars, because the weather equipment pushes onto the belts.

Chrome internal door locks were fitted until 1971, with anti-burst door locks after this point. If you close the door slowly you will notice a double click; the internal locking lever will only move when the lock/door is in this double clicked position.

## Carpets                                                    4  3  2  1
Check the carpets. Are they wet, stained, moth damaged, threadbare or faded? Is there evidence of rodent damage? Rubber matting was fitted on the inside of the bulkhead until 1989, since when carpet has been fitted. Slide the seat forward and look at the carpet underneath. Rear spring hanger leather may be damaged where the seat has been slid back. There should be a heel mat on the driver's side front footwell carpet. The front crossmember in front of the seat may be carpeted, have a stainless cover, or be exposed. Two carpet pieces have been supplied with new cars since 1998 to cover the crossmember on each side (these are not factory-fitted to allow the chassis number to be clearly seen for export purposes). The rear luggage compartment carpet should be a single piece, extending down either side of the propshaft. On some retrims this carpet may have an upper and lower section. If this is the case check the rest of the interior for fit, and compare it to other similar aged examples for originality.

## Dashboard and steering wheel                               4  3  2  1
There have been various dashboard designs over the decades. Leather or vinyl covered dashboards were standard from 1971 until 2004. Walnut dashboards have always been a popular option, being introduced as a factory option from 1988; these were supplied with lockable lids, so check the lock works. A finger tab under the lock was removed in 1998 to meet European regulations. Check the condition

The dashboard layout from 1976-1986.

Dashboard as fitted 1986-1997, with centre panel covered in leather.

Dashboard and interior as seen on the late 1997-2003 long door models.

Custom dashboard and gauges fitted to a Le Mans 62, showing unique instruments, St Christopher badge and Moto-Lita steering wheel.

Dashboard from 2003 until the end of production.

of the dashboard for bleaching and cracks, and examine the crash padding material (fitted from 1971) for ring damage.

Original dashboards are often upgraded by owners to either a walnut finish or one with a different layout.

Only three styles of steering wheel have been used since 1968: these were a black-rimmed, 15in steering wheel fitted as standard, but the no-cost option of a 14in rim was also a popular choice. Post-1998 steering wheels have a padded centre with the horn push in the middle. A lot of owners change to a Moto-Lita steering wheel, ideally fitted to the Moto-Lita boss. There is very little effect on the steering between a 15in or 14in wheel. If a 13in wheel is fitted however, the steering will be a little heavier.

Check the steering wheel for excessive movement and play. Some owners pull on the steering wheel as they get in and out, which can prematurely wear the top column bushes.

Airbags were an expensive cost option from 1998 and are quite rare. Airbag steering wheels are 16in in diameter, and the passenger airbag is mounted in the glovebox behind a cover. Cars fitted with airbags are sought for export as some countries stipulate them as a condition of entry.

Steering columns have been adjustable from 1998, and are generally kept in the uppermost position. Some cars may have had an aftermarket modification to allow the column to tilt a little higher.

## Dashboard electrics and gauges       1

From 1969-1977, there were two centrally mounted Smiths gauges, one containing the speedometer, and a cluster gauge that included temperature ammeter, fuel and oil gauges. Large rocker switches were fitted. Check all the switches work; the hazard switch sometimes sticks due to lack of use, or causes issues with the indicators.

The next layout continued until 1986, with the speedometer and rev counter in easy view. The warning light cluster between the gauges was from a Jaguar XJ-S. The oil pressure gauge, voltmeter, temperature and fuel gauges were fitted in a row in the middle of the dashboard, with a series of dashboard switches mounted

Cream instruments were fitted from 2003: the panel usually has push-button switches, but this one has been updated to toggles for a period look.

below. The Lucas rocker switches can now be quite fragile due to age, and are expensive to replace. Exact originals are now very hard to find.

In 1986 the switches changed to VDO, which are very reliable, and the warning light cluster changed to individual lamps. The gauges from this age sometimes mist up, but holes were drilled into their backs in the early 1990s to help with this. Fuel gauges are known to be quite unreliable as the fuel tank sender unit is mounted in a tube. The gauge may read just over ¾ tank when full but will read empty accurately.

Digital display speedometers are fitted from 1996-2004. These can suffer due to damp/age, and the displays may stop working intermittently. Common issues to look out for are flickering, scrolling of the numbers, or the display going out altogether. Dry, warm weather conditions can restore the unit in some instances. At the time of writing these units cannot be repaired, and exact matches are unavailable, but similar speedo head units can be purchased. Any speedometer change should be noted in the vehicle history with the mileage at the point of change. Look out for split sealing rubbers which can cause the gauges to work loose on their mounting plates.

Long-door cars from 1998 have the dashboard further back and mounted vertically to allow for the option of airbags. The demister pipes were removed to enable this, and a heated windscreen was fitted. The centre cluster has four gauges, and the switches are mounted in two groups, one on either side of the speedometer and rev counter, instead of underneath. With a 14in steering wheel the speedometer can be a little difficult to read.

The dashboard layout changed again in 2002, with the Le Mans 62 cars changing to cream dials; this was continued until the end of production.

Start the car and check all gauges and dashboard warning lights work. On 2003-2004 cars, with cream dials, ensure the indicators and hazard lamps work – water ingress in the indicator lamps can cause a short circuit that damages the instrument panel circuit board, which is expensive to replace. The switches are push buttons, the fan switch on cars from 2003-2004 may only have one speed rather than two. The chrome gauge rims can split or badly tarnish.

Special editions often have different dashboard finishes and layouts, and some owners may have changed earlier gauges to cream faces or changed switches to Jaguar style toggle switches.

Check wiper and indicator stalks for security and operation, and test the windscreen washers – washer jet tubes can become detached and jets become clogged.

## Interior controls including pedals  ④ ③ ② ①
Ensure that all controls work. Clutch and brake pedals should have rubbers fitted, or have an anti-slip finish. The rubbers sometimes fall off, and if the brake pedal rubber is missing that is a UK MOT failure item. Clutch pedal springs can break and clevis pins can wear, so check for excessive 'slop' in the pedals. Check the radio works, remembering to pull up the aerial if necessary; electric aerials are rare.

## Heater controls  ④ ③ ② ①
Heaters were fitted as standard from 1972. Check heater controls work and that flaps on the heater box move. Earlier cars have a pull cable to operate the heater valve, this is rarely used so ensure it hasn't seized up. Later cars have a turn knob on the heater box. The newer the car the better the heater operation. Heated seats have become a popular option in recent years and can be retro-fitted, though they take some time to warm up. Check these with the engine running.

## Keys and immobilisers  ④ ③ ② ①
Each lock has its own key, so the fuel cap, door, and glovebox keys will all be different. Fuel cap keys are LF keys (easy to remember as 'lead free'); door and glovebox keys are FS keys.

A standard Rover ignition lock was fitted from 1971 to 1997. From late 1997 a new type of lock was used and the car was supplied with an immobiliser key fob. The immobiliser self arms after a couple of minutes – you'll see a red dash lamp in the middle instrument cluster that flashes to confirm the system is active. To disarm the system, press the button on the fob before putting the key in the ignition. It takes a few moments for the system to deactivate, so racing starts should be avoided. Once disarmed, put the 'ignition' on, allow the fuel pump to buzz and build up pressure, then start the car – otherwise you may find the system hasn't deactivated properly: it will crank but the engine will not fire. The fob works on a number scroll, so if the red light does not change when you press the blank button, you may need to press it up to five times as it scrolls through the numbers. The relay behind the dashboard will then click and the light will go out. On some later cars putting the key in the ignition can deactivate the immobiliser, but this may not work on every car.

Earlier Plus 8s (pre-1982) may need to be cranked over for a few seconds, to allow oil pressure to build up before the ignition is given a feed via a pressure switch. We have known this switch to fail on occasions.

Keys from a later Plus 8 with immobiliser fob.

Each new car would have been originally supplied with two ignition keys, two fuel cap keys, two door keys, and two glovebox keys if a walnut dashboard was fitted. If the passenger side has a lock an additional two keys would have been supplied. Ensure all door and glovebox keys fit and work.

## Wiper ⁴ ³ ² ¹ operation and blades

Check the wipers and washers work on all speeds, and that pre-1998 stalks are not loose in the switch housing. Post-1998 switches are very reliable. Washer pumps and jets can block up with sediment from washer fluid due to lack of use. The wipers are best described as 'adequate.' Check the wiper blade rubbers for splitting. Make sure the wipers park in the lower position when turned off, as the motor park switches can fail.

## Wheels ⁴ ³ ² ¹ and tyres

The different wheels were discussed in chapter 7. Examine the wheels for kerb damage and general appearance. Loose spokes are not usually an issue on later cars with wire wheels. The stainless wheels on the Le Mans and very late models are easy to maintain, and can be

Early LT77 five-speed gear knob. The 'fly off' handbrake is clearly shown, and one of the positions at which radios can be fitted.

The later R380 gear knob, with the handbrake now on the right.

cleaned with a power washer. A stainless wheel will have a slight creamy/yellow look in the reflection, whereas a chrome rim or wheel nut will have a whiter reflection.

The tyres of wire-wheeled cars from 1998 sometimes rub on the inside face of the superform front wings when on lock. You will spot a polished section on the inside of the wing if the wheel has rubbed.

The rear wheels on early cars are not central in the wheelarch. Be careful if you run your hand over the wheel, as you can trap your fingers.

Check tyres carefully for age related cracks. If they are over ten years old they need changing regardless of appearance. Morgans are good on tyre wear, though hardening and flat-spotting due to lack of use are common, especially on the 14in

The wiper stalk was mounted on the left from 1976 until the long door was introduced. This car also has a Moto Lita steering wheel.

The wiper stalk, with intermittent wipe, swapped sides with the indicator stalk on the long door models. The steering column cover also changed.

alloy wheels. This can cause a serious front scuttle vibration. Look out for this on the road test.

### Rear suspension and brakes

Leaf springs are fitted to the rear, two-seaters having five-leaf as standard. These can sag quite quickly, so six-leafs have been a popular option.

Lever arm shock absorbers were standard fit until 1992, when they changed over to a telescopic shock absorber arrangement mounted on a brace bar that helps to stiffen the chassis. If you're able to lift out the rear luggage board on pre-2003 cars, you'll see the axle and rear suspension. This is ideal for a quick check of the shock absorbers.

Have a look at the handbrake linkage and the rear brake back plates. The paper gaskets can weep, but wetness here could also be a sign of hub seal failure. Later BTR axles (post-1996) are less prone to hub seal leaks.

1968-1976 alloy wheel.

1976-1982 14in alloy wheel.

The alloy wheel from 1982 onwards.

A centre lock alloy wheel.

A 1994-on optional chrome wire wheel.

2002 Le Mans/35th Anniversary 16in stainless wire wheel.

Rear brakes went from manual adjustment (Girling) to self adjusting (AP) brakes in 1993, while the fly-off handbrake moved from the left side to the right. On earlier models you should be able to pull up the handbrake three clicks for it to lock in place. On later cars there is more movement, so four-five clicks is normal to the locking position. You should not hear the clicks during normal application of the handbrake, as it prematurely wears out the ratchet. The correct method for applying the handbrake is as follows: pull the lever back towards you until you have a fair bit

of tension, push the button on the top, move the lever forward, you will then feel the handbrake lock in place. To release, pull the lower part of the lever towards you, the spring loaded button will pop up, and the lever will then travel easily towards the front of the car (hence the term 'fly-off'). The levers can rub on the handbrake gaiter, so you may need to assist it to the fully off position.

Turn on the ignition and check that the warning light goes out. Rear wheel cylinders are prone to leaking and seizure on post-93 cars. If they are seized, and the car is on level ground, try to push the car backwards and forwards. You may feel the rear brakes grab, or the car could be very hard to push. It's common for the rear brakes to pass a UK MOT even with sticking cylinders. Subsequent removal of the drums will enable you to assess the cylinders. If there is no record of cylinder changes in the service history, you may need to budget for this. At the dealership we have to put new cylinders on over 70 per cent of the later cars we sell during handover preparation.

Note: on pre-1976 cars the handbrake cable end is soldered on, and if you pull too hard on the lever you can pull the end off.

## Exhaust

Over time the Plus 8 has regularly changed from single to dual exhaust systems. This area can be a bit of a minefield, as it's quite common to find aftermarket systems have been fitted. In particular Librands crossover dual systems have been a popular upgrade on 1990s cars.

The first 50 cars in 1968 had a single system with a balance pipe between the downpipes. In 1971 the exhaust changed to a dual system again with a balance pipe. In 1977 four branch manifolds were fitted with a dual system, including a main silencer and small rear box on each side. In late 1986 a single system was fitted with three inline silencer boxes. In 1990 the dual system returned without catalytic converters until 1992, when they were fitted to meet regulations. The system went back to a single system until 1997. In 1997 the system changed back to a dual exhaust, manufactured from stainless steel as a standard factory

Exhausts vary from single to twin systems; some downpipes go through the valance.

Some downpipes pass through the chassis.

Catalytic converters were fitted from 1992: this is a 1996 single system with twin cats.

fit, rather than the earlier mild steel systems. This design continued until the end of production.

The catalytic converters are stainless, but have steel flanges and clamps which can corrode badly as they are behind the front wheel and thus exposed to the elements. The flanges can be replaced to prolong the life of the catalyst. Be wary of cars that have had catalytic converters removed or changed to a sports cat. These can be harder to get through emission testing.

Centre boxes can crack where the pipework enters and exits the silencer, baffles can work loose, and exhaust mountings split with age.

Some of the aftermarket exhausts cross underneath the sump, and the pipes are not completely sealed so they can 'chuff' when cold. This can cause issues on emission tests, where the system fails until it's fully warm. If the car has the plastic oiler pipes still in place, be careful of idling and revving when stationary for long periods. We have known the pipes to melt and drip oil onto a red hot exhaust.

Main silencers are mounted under the wing. 'Cotton reel' mounts were usually used, but often split with age. Most systems are now stainless steel.

Rear tailpipes can be straight through or have an additional small silencer box.

## Front suspension

The Morgan sliding pillar arrangement is legendary. Dating back to 1909, every Plus 8 in this book uses it.

The stub axle is fitted with an upper and lower bush, and slides on the kingpin. A mainspring is fitted above the stub axle, and a rebound spring below. Check the springs are not broken, and that the stub axle rests on the rebound spring. All Plus

Morgan's famous sliding pillar kingpin assembly, showing track rod end, adjustable shock absorber, rebound spring and aftermarket roller bearing kit, which removes the need for the damper blade assembly.

8s until 2004 have a bronze thrust plate between the main spring and stub axle base. If this is not lubricated properly the steering can become very tight. The thin damper blade behind absorbs some of the shock going through the system. This sometimes needs adjusting on service, and can click when the steering is turned. In cars produced until 2000 you will find an oiler valve, which releases engine oil via a thin pipe to the top of the kingpins. Every 500-750 miles the valve should be pressed when the engine is started and while still cold, but not all owners use this system, and it was phased out in 2000. Additional grease nipples are fitted to grease the suspension more regularly.

Aftermarket roller bearings replacing the thrust plates can be fitted on earlier cars. These improve the self-centring of the steering. If you're able to safely raise the front of the car (ideally on axle stands) you can check wheel bearing play, kingpin wear, and play in the track rod ends.

With the front wheel directly in front of you, hold it at the 1 o'clock and 7 o'clock positions to check for movement. You may feel a small amount of play – this could just be in the wheel bearing. Next, hold the wheel at 11 o'clock and 5 o'clock positions and check for movement. Finally, hold the wheel at 6 o'clock position, and pull it back and forth. Watch the tyre as you move it. You should have no more than ½in (13mm) movement at the bottom. If there is play, movement will be noticeable, and you may even hear a 'clonk.' Get the vendor to assist so you can check behind the wheel at the stub axle for movement.

Check the track rod ends for play by holding the front wheel at 9 o'clock and 3 o'clock positions. I have found that, with the car back on the ground, gripping and rocking the top of the wheel to check for kingpin wear is pointless, unless the bushes are very badly worn (you would probably have noticed uneven tyre wear if this was the case – evident as wear on the outside of the tread, similar to having too much positive camber). A little movement in the kingpins does not mean they need changing immediately, they could last several thousand more miles.

Various types of kingpins are available, including stainless steel and hardened chrome. There are many opinions on which type to fit, and whether you should grease or use the oiler valve. At this stage all you are looking for is excessive play and whether you will need a front end overhaul in the next few years. Some cars may have the increasingly popular option of the Suplex/SSL front suspension. This has adjustable platforms and springs to allow more progressive spring and suspension travel, and can improve ride, particularly over potholes. Adjustable shock absorbers are also a popular upgrade.

## Front brakes

Given the age range of cars covered by this book, the front brakes will likely be non-vented disc brakes. Although harder to check on steel-wheeled cars, look at the brake discs for scoring, 'blueing' of the contact surface (this indicates excessive heat from sticking caliper pistons) and for wear lips. Look from behind the wheel to check the inner faces of the discs, they can become quite pitted with rust. Discs are a Morgan-only part, but can be skimmed if there is only light wear.

Later cars with very low mileage can develop brake disc judder. Check for this on the road test.

Servo assistance was not standard until late 1992, so the brake pedal may feel harder on non-servo cars and more pedal effort may be needed to stop. Visually check the brake hoses on lock-to-lock for condition and fouling.

## Steering

The early cars were fitted with a Burman steering box, replaced by a Gemmer steering box in 1984. Check for leaks and a smooth operation. The steering wheel will have a bit of play in the straight ahead position, but there's less detectable play on a Gemmer box. Gemmer boxes are a popular upgrade on much earlier cars.

Rack and pinion steering was offered as an option in 1984, and became standard in 1985. Check operation for smoothness, ask the seller to wiggle the steering wheel from side-to-side so you can check steering joints between the column to the rack, and for excessive play in the rack. Rack gaiters split and are quite expensive to replace, as are the rack end caps.

During the wiggle test, check for excess movement in the track rod joints.

The Gemmer steering box was a popular conversion from the early Burman steering boxes.

The inner steering rack joints may show signs of wear, while track rod gaiters can split with age, and are now a UK MOT failure point.

### Tool kit

4 3 2 1

The tool kit should consist of a jack with handle, hammer, and a spanner for wire-wheeled cars. If the car has alloy wheels the tool kit includes a jack with handle and a wheel wrench. Until 2003 the tool kit was mounted in the tool box, on the bulkhead under the right-hand bonnet, but after that it was situated in a felt-lined tray under a thin board on the luggage shelf area behind the seats. Check the tray for impact damage from the axle. During the 1980s and 1990s the jack and tools were wrapped in brown parcel paper, and you may find cars with the tools still in their original paper.

### Exterior lights

4 3 2 1

Check that all lights work. Bad earth connections are common. Indicator lens

High level brake light introduced in 1998 as one of 114 changes to the car to meet new European type approval regulations.

locating lugs should face downwards, and not be visible when looking down onto the car. This is a clear pointer to a possible paint repair or a previous wiring issue.

Headlamps should match. Lucus sealed beam units were used until 1981, Cibie from approximately 1982-1986, Lucas H4 units to 1995, and Wipac headlamp units from 1995 (these can mist and go milky inside, but replacements are cheap). For cars from 1998 ensure the rear foglight works, and the switch illuminates. On all Plus 8s check for hazard, foglight, spot lamps, and reverse light operation if present.

Spot lamps were a standard item from 1969 through to 1997, with Lucas LR6 from 1969 to 1977, Lumax until 1997, and Marchal lamps 1984-1985. Lumax and Marchal lamps are becoming hard to source. Check spot lamp location on early cars, as they were mounted directly onto the wings and can come away over time due to metal fatigue. On later cars, L-shaped brackets became a popular alternative for mounting the lamps.

### Right-hand engine bay

With the bonnet open, check the condition of the top of the bulkhead, inside the toolbox if fitted, fuse box area, inner valance, chassis crossmember, wiring and hoses. Check overall engine bay and exhaust condition. Is it clean and tidy or does it look neglected? Light oxidisation of aluminium castings is to be expected. Recheck for evidence of overspray.

1969 Plus 8 engine bay: note the curved rocker cover and remote brake servo.

1982 engine bay.

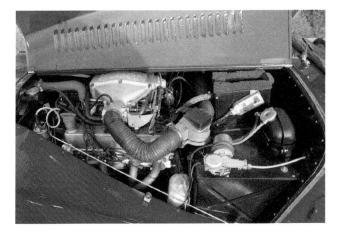

3.5 LE injection engine bay.

3.9 14CUX injection engine bay.

## Left-hand engine bay

As per the right-hand side, check the engine components, bulkhead, valance and exhaust for condition, and score accordingly.

## Cooling system

Check the coolant level when the engine is switched off and cold, either via the main radiator cap or from the expansion bottle. There is a coolant level tab in the metal expansion bottles, and providing there is coolant in the tank it should be fine. You may need to shine a torch to see the reflection of the coolant. The level can settle below the tab level as the system will find its natural point. If the tank is empty, check the level in the radiator.

Ask when the antifreeze was last changed. Blue antifreeze is normal on all Plus 8s, but you will find the odd exception. Blue antifreeze can go 'milky' with age, and clog up the radiator tubes. Head gaskets rarely fail, so a flush and replenish should be all that is required.

4.6 14CUX engine bay.

4.0 GEMs injection engine bay.

Check with a mirror or by hand around the water pump, as these can leak. Are there any drips, or coolant sitting in the inlet manifold valley gasket? It could be a hose or housing leak.

Look out for radiator leaks as part of your engine bay check. Auxiliary belt squeals can be caused by antifreeze ingress from a previous leaking radiator or hose: the multi ribbed serpentine belts are prone to this.

## Battery

The battery is mounted behind the left-hand front seat, and is accessible by an access panel under the rear board. If a sealed gel-type battery is fitted, these are located on the bulkhead in the engine bay. Access for changing and checking the battery can be tricky.

A gel-sealed battery was fitted from 2002; these are expensive and may only last as little as two years if not regularly used/charged. Morgan went back to a standard type battery in October 2005 after Plus 8 production finished. Batteries run down if the car is not used, so connecting to a battery conditioner is recommended.

A cigar lighter socket/auxiliary socket is an ideal connection point due to the location of the battery and the fact it is permanently live. (Cigar lighters were optional on the earlier cars and usually mounted in the glovebox.)

Battery conditioners are plugged in and left on the car to keep the battery fully charged. However, their use can disguise the true state of a battery over five years old, and when disconnected the battery could go flat very quickly. Check the history/ask the vendor to provide proof if the car has had a recent battery change.

A red isolator switch was fitted as standard from around 1986 until 1999. When the red key is turned and removed it disconnects the battery: a handy theft deterrent and battery preserver. These are not recommended on the very late cars, though, because the car may run rough until it has completed a drive cycle, and the ECU feed will be interrupted if the red key is switched off.

Note: clocks are analogue, so will drain the battery. Also, old radio headsets can cause a large current drain.

## Clutch

All Plus 8 clutches are hydraulically operated. Pedals can wear, and it's common for the rubbers to fall off. The clutch should have a smooth pedal action with the bite point just over halfway, and no sponginess. The cars aren't prone to clutch slip or judder, and the clutches rarely wear out, despite most owners lightly resting their foot on the pedal. Some release bearing noise is to be expected, which will quieten once the pedal is depressed. Some light gearbox bearing noise can normally be heard as there is very little soundproofing.

## Under bonnet brakes

Check brake fluid level and condition of the master cylinder. Brake pipe routing should be neat and tidy. Reservoirs sometimes have heat shields to protect them from heat damage on Librands exhaust systems and on later cars.

## Engine, gearbox and axle

Complete your visual inspection of the engine: check the level and cleanliness of the oil, and the engine mount brackets for cracks and missing bolts. Start the car and listen for abnormal or chuffing noises from the exhaust manifolds.

Look underneath the car to check for fluid leaks, As mentioned, the undersides are rarely dry. The fifth-speed rear gearbox gaskets usually leak, and front pinion seals, drain plugs and axle pan cover gaskets can leak to a degree. A heavy deposit of oil over the middle of the fuel tank/boards, viewed from underneath, can indicate that the axle has run low of oil. It's worth checking for dampness and staining

Five-speed LT77 gearbox. The silver fifth-speed housing gaskets usually weep.

around the fuel tank and for strong fuel smells. Fuel tanks on older cars can leak at the seams and the fuel filler hoses can perish badly on later cars.

Rear axle, also showing battery location.

## Test drive
If all is good so far, it's now test drive time.

### Cold start
☐ ☐ ☐ ☐

Start the car. Carburettor cars can be a bit lumpy on choke, make sure the car idles, and pick up the revs to check for misfires. Does the car run well from cold? Listen for rattles and abnormal noises as you pull away. On hotwire injection models check the car moves smoothly from the cold start cycle to the warm cycle; misfires and hesitations have been known to occur. This can be caused by a breakdown of the ECU circuits or wiring pin issues; it's tricky to pinpoint but luckily quite rare.

### Gearbox operation
☐ ☐ ☐ ☐

All the gearboxes have a short throw and positive change across a narrow gate. There is so much torque that first gear isn't required. Make sure the lever doesn't feel sloppy – the LT77 early five-speed gearboxes have an extension housing which has rubber bushes, which can break down with age. The lever is also held in place by a cup with a 10mm bolt, the bolt location tab can break off, altering the gearlever feel and causing a rattle. The five-speed gearboxes may feel notchy and could crunch in 2nd gear for the first half a mile while the oil circulates and warms up. Synchros can wear, too, so ensure you go up and down the gearbox, check the operation and listen for abnormal noises while driving and changing gear. Generally the gearboxes are strong and will cover many miles before requiring serious attention. Don't forget to check reverse gear.

### Steering
☐ ☐ ☐ ☐

You will get a lot of feel and feedback through the steering, there will be some straight ahead play with steering box cars, racks are more precise. It will feel heavier at lower speed or when manoeuvring, as they do not have power steering. It should have the same feel side-to-side. A rubbing sound on full lock is normally due to the tyre rubbing on the block mounted on the chassis. Check for wheel shake at 50-60mph, which could be due to incorrect wheel balance. Progressive vibration through the steering or strange handling could be flat-spotted tyres.

## Noises, clonks, rattles and squeaks

Listen out for the following:

• Creak/squeak from behind the seats. This is usually due to the front rear spring bushes being dried out: lubrication is all that is needed.

• A light 'clonk' as you pull away is normal on the old GKN axles, being take-up in the prop and diff. This is quite normal. There shouldn't be a clonk with the later axles.

• Loud whines from the five-speed gearboxes and whooshing noises increasing in pitch with speed can indicate gearbox and axle bearing noise. Moss/four-speed gearboxes have their own distinctive noise as standard.

• A click from the wheel area as you pull away can mean wire wheels have not been tightened sufficiently on the hubs, and the wheel is moving on the spline – this is common if an owner has removed the wheels to clean them.

• Sidescreens rattle and can squeak against the elbow panel.

• Luggage rack bars and exhausts can rattle. Minor adjustment may be all that's required.

• Creaking from the front. The upper wing stays can break and cause a creak whilst driving.

• A whistling noise from the windscreen area could be the screen, and headlamp rims can cause a loud whistle.

• Lever arm shock absorbers are noisy in operation compared to telescopic shocks.

• Noisy fan belts can be caused by antifreeze dropping onto the belt from a previous radiator leak, so recheck this area after the road test.

• Rotational clonking/scraping noise from the rear when cornering can, in some instances, be the propshaft rubbing on the surrounding housing.

## Performance and handling

You should be pleasantly surprised by the ride; it's not as hard as people sometimes claim. It's often said that it feels like you're travelling 10mph faster than you actually are. The car should pull sweetly with plenty of torque in all gears; tuned examples can be quite noisy and harder to drive. Injection cars, especially the 4.6s that have had chip upgrades, can feel very smooth and responsive. Compared to a 4/4 or Plus 4, the Plus 8 can feel heavier at the front end when cornering and driving in a spirited fashion. Many owners prefer this feeling as the car feels rooted on the road.

Check for drifting to one side, particularly when braking; sticking calipers or even under-inflated tyres can cause this. Check for vibration through the brake pedal: this may be due to warped brake discs. Some things may take a little getting used to, such as non-servo brakes, the lack of ABS, and the way the pedals come up from the floor.

The car should feel predictable and stable. If not it will need further investigation. Please remember it will feel like a cross between a 1960s classic and a modern car; this is part of its charm.

## Instruments

Check that all instruments work as they should, particularly the temperature and fuel gauges. If there is a digital display check it's displaying clearly. Make sure they're not misted. The oil gauges can move through quite a range, check the needle isn't going straight over to maximum (the sensor can short internally), but issues with poor oil pressure are rare. Do the indicators self cancel? Engine temperature should be between 85-105 degrees C while driving. Are any warning lights illuminated? Does the speedometer needle read smoothly and display the correct speed and miles travelled?

## Final hot checks

I hope you have enjoyed your road test. Now, with the engine idling, recheck the temperature gauge, under the bonnets for leaks and for smoke from the exhaust. Leave the engine running until the coolant fan kicks in; this is usually just over 100-105 degrees C; once it cuts out again turn the engine off.

If you noticed any pulling or drifting on the steering carefully check each wheel for temperature by placing your hand on the centre hub. They should all be about the same. Leave for a few minutes and then restart the car to ensure it will start when hot, and to recheck the engine bay in case you've missed anything. Turn off the engine one last time and then evaluate your scores

## Evaluation procedure

Add up the total points.

Score: 160 = excellent; 120 = good; 80 = average; 40 = poor.

Cars scoring over 112 will be completely usable and will require only maintenance and care to preserve condition. Cars scoring between 40 and 82 will require some serious work (at much the same cost regardless of score). Cars scoring between 83 and 111 will require very careful assessment of the necessary repair/restoration costs in order to arrive at a realistic value.

# 10 Auctions
– sold! Another way to buy your dream

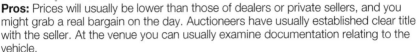

## Auction pros & cons

**Pros:** Prices will usually be lower than those of dealers or private sellers, and you might grab a real bargain on the day. Auctioneers have usually established clear title with the seller. At the venue you can usually examine documentation relating to the vehicle.

**Cons:** You have to rely on a sketchy catalogue description of condition and history. The opportunity to inspect is limited and you cannot drive the car. Auction cars are often a little below par and may require some work. It's easy to overbid. There will usually be a buyer's premium to pay in addition to the auction hammer price.

## Which auction?

Auctions by established auctioneers are advertised in car magazines and on the auction houses' websites. A catalogue, or a simple printed list of the lots for auctions might only be available a day or two ahead, though often lots are listed and pictured on auctioneers' websites much earlier. Contact the auction company to ask if previous auction selling prices are available as this is useful information (details of past sales are often available on websites).

## Catalogue, entry fee and payment details

When you purchase the catalogue of the vehicles in the auction, it often acts as a ticket allowing two people to attend the viewing days and the auction. Catalogue details tend to be comparatively brief, but will include information such as 'one owner from new, low mileage, full service history,' etc. It will also usually show a guide price to give you some idea of what to expect to pay, and will tell you what is charged as a 'Buyer's premium.' The catalogue will also contain details of acceptable forms of payment. At the fall of the hammer an immediate deposit is usually required, the balance payable within 24 hours. If the plan is to pay by cash there may be a cash limit. Some auctions will accept payment by debit card. Sometimes credit or charge cards are acceptable, but will often incur an extra charge. A bank draft or bank transfer will have to be arranged in advance with your own bank as well as with the auction house. No car will be released before all payments are cleared. If delays occur in payment transfers then storage costs can accrue.

## Buyer's premium

A buyer's premium will be added to the hammer price: don't forget this in your calculations. It is not usual for there to be a further state tax or local tax on the purchase price and/or on the buyer's premium.

## Viewing

In some instances it's possible to view on the day, or days before, as well as in the hours prior to, the auction. There are auction officials available who are willing to help out by opening engine and luggage compartments and to allow you to inspect the interior. While the officials may start the engine for you, a test drive is out of the question. Crawling under and around the car as much as you want is permitted, but you can't suggest that the car you are interested in be jacked up, or attempt to do the job yourself. You can also ask to see any documentation available.

## Bidding

Before you take part in the auction, decide your maximum bid – and stick to it!

It may take a while for the auctioneer to reach the lot you are interested in, so use that time to observe how other bidders behave. When it's the turn of your car, attract the auctioneer's attention and make an early bid. The auctioneer will then look to you for a reaction every time another bid is made, usually the bids will be in fixed increments until the bidding slows, when smaller increments will often be accepted before the hammer falls. If you want to withdraw from the bidding, make sure the auctioneer understands your intentions – a vigorous shake of the head when he or she looks to you for the next bid should do the trick! Assuming that you are the successful bidder, the auctioneer will note your card or paddle number, and from that moment on you will be responsible for the vehicle. If the car is unsold, either because it failed to reach the reserve or because there was little interest, it may be possible to negotiate with the owner, via the auctioneers, after the sale is over.

## Successful bid

There are two more items to think about. How to get the car home, and insurance. If you can't drive the car, your own or a hired trailer is one way, another is to have the vehicle shipped using the facilities of a local company. The auction house will also have details of companies specialising in the transfer of cars.

Insurance for immediate cover can usually be purchased on site, but it may be more cost-effective to make arrangements with your own insurance company in advance, and then call to confirm the full details.

## eBay & other online auctions?

eBay or other online auctions could land you a car at a bargain price, though you'd be foolhardy to bid without examining the car first, something most vendors encourage. A useful feature of eBay is that the geographical location of the car is shown, so you can narrow your choices to those within a realistic radius of home. Be prepared to be outbid in the last few moments of the auction. Remember, your bid is binding and that it will be very, very difficult to get restitution in the case of a crooked vendor fleecing you – caveat emptor!

Be aware that some cars offered for sale in online auctions are 'ghost' cars. Don't part with any cash without being sure that the vehicle does actually exist and is as described (usually pre-bidding inspection is possible).

## Auctioneers

Barrett-Jackson www.barrett-jackson.com / Bonhams www.bonhams.com / British Car Auctions (BCA) www.bca-europe.com or www.british-car-auctions.co.uk / Cheffins www.cheffins.co.uk / Christies www.christies.com / Coys www.coys.co.uk / eBay www.eBay.com / H&H www.classic-auctions.co.uk / RM www.rmauctions.com / Shannons www.shannons.com.au / Silver www.silverauctions.com – to name but a few.

# 11 Paperwork

– correct documentation is essential!

## The paper trail

Classic, collector and prestige cars usually come with a large portfolio of paperwork accumulated and passed on by a succession of proud owners. This documentation represents the real history of the car and from it can be deduced the level of care the car has received, how much it's been used, which specialists have worked on it and the dates of major repairs and restorations. All of this information will be priceless to you as the new owner, so be very wary of cars with little paperwork to support their claimed history.

## Registration documents

All countries/states have some form of registration for private vehicles whether it's like the American 'pink slip' system or the British 'log book' system.

It is essential to check that the registration document is genuine, that it relates to the car in question, and that all the vehicle's details are correctly recorded, including chassis/VIN and engine numbers (if these are shown). If you are buying from the previous owner, his or her name and address will be recorded in the document: this will not be the case if you are buying from a dealer.

In the UK the current (Euro-aligned) registration document is named 'V5C,' and is printed in coloured sections of blue, green and pink. The blue section relates to the car specification, the green section has details of the new owner and the pink section is sent to the DVLA in the UK when the car is sold. A small section in yellow deals with selling the car within the motor trade.

## Previous ownership records

Due to the introduction of important new legislation on data protection, it is no longer possible to acquire, from the British DVLA, a list of previous owners of a car

A typical service history.

you own, or are intending to purchase. This scenario will also apply to dealerships and other specialists, from who you may wish to make contact and acquire information on previous ownership and work carried out.

If the car has a foreign registration, there may be expensive and time-consuming formalities to complete. Do you really want the hassle?

## Roadworthiness certificate
Most country/state administrations require that vehicles are regularly tested to prove that they are safe to use on the public highway and do not produce excessive emissions. In the UK that test (the 'MOT') is carried out at approved testing stations, for a fee. In the USA the requirement varies, but most states insist on an emissions test every two years as a minimum, while the police are charged with pulling over unsafe-looking vehicles.

In the UK the test is required on an annual basis once a vehicle becomes three years old. Of particular relevance for older cars is that the certificate issued includes the mileage reading recorded at the test date and, therefore, becomes an independent record of that car's history. Ask the seller if previous certificates are available. Without an MOT the vehicle should be trailered to its new home, unless you insist that a valid MOT is part of the deal. (Not such a bad idea this, as at least you will know the car was roadworthy on the day it was tested and you don't need to wait for the old certificate to expire before having the test done.)

In the UK, vehicles over 40 years old on May 20th each year are exempt from MOT testing. Owners can still have the test carried out if they so wish.

## Road licence
The administration of every country/state charges some kind of tax for the use of its road system, the actual form of the 'road licence' and how it is displayed, varying enormously country to country and state to state.

Whatever the form of the 'road licence' it must relate to the vehicle carrying it, and must be present and valid if the car is to be driven legally on the public highway.

Changed legislation in the UK means that the seller of a car must surrender any existing road fund licence, and it is the responsibility of the new owner to re-tax the vehicle at the time of purchase and before the car can be driven on the road. It's therefore vital to see the Vehicle Registration Certificate (V5C) at the time of purchase, and to have access to the New Keeper Supplement (V5C/2), allowing the buyer to obtain road tax immediately.

In the UK, classic vehicles 40 years old or more, on the 1st January each year get free road tax. It is still necessary to renew the tax status every year, even if there is no change.

If the car is untaxed because it has not been used for a period of time, the owner has to inform the licensing authorities.

## Certificates of authenticity
For many makes of collectible car it is possible to get a certificate proving the age and authenticity (eg engine and chassis numbers, paint colour and trim) of a particular vehicle, these are sometimes called 'Heritage Certificates' and if the car comes with one of these it is a definite bonus. If you want to obtain one, Morgan Motor Company is able to prove a certificate for a fee. See the main factory website, 'Chassis records' – see https://www.morgan-motor.com/chassis-records/

If the car has been used in European classic car rallies it may have a FIVA (Fédération International des Véhicules Anciens) certificate. The so-called 'FIVA Passport,' or 'FIVA Vehicle Identity Card,' enables organisers and participants to recognise whether or not a particular vehicle is suitable for individual events. If you want to obtain such a certificate go to www.fbhvc.co.uk or www.fiva.org. There will be similar organisations in other countries too.

## Valuation certificate

Hopefully, the vendor will have a recent valuation certificate, or letter signed by a recognised expert stating how much he, or she, believes the particular car to be worth (such documents, together with photos, are usually needed to get 'agreed value' insurance). Generally such documents should act only as confirmation of your own assessment of the car rather than a guarantee of value as the expert has probably not seen the car in the flesh. The easiest way to find out how to obtain a formal valuation is to contact the owners' club.

## Service history

Although mainly serviced and repaired by dealers and specialist garages, some cars will have been serviced at home by enthusiastic (and hopefully capable) owners for a good number of years. Nevertheless, try to obtain as much service history and other paperwork pertaining to the car as you can. Naturally, dealer stamps, or specialist garage receipts score most points in the value stakes. However, anything helps in the great authenticity game, items like the original bill of sale, handbook, parts invoices and repair bills, adding to the story and the character of the car. Even a brochure correct to the year of the car's manufacture is a useful document and something that you could well have to search hard to locate in future years. If the seller claims that the car has been restored, then expect receipts and other evidence from a specialist restorer.

If the seller claims to have carried out regular servicing, ask what work was completed, when, and seek some evidence of it being carried out. Your assessment of the car's overall condition should tell you whether the seller's claims are genuine.

## Restoration photographs

If the seller tells you that the car has been restored, then expect to be shown a series of photographs taken while the restoration was under way. Pictures taken at various stages, and from various angles, should help you gauge the thoroughness of the work. If you buy the car, ask if you can have all the photographs as they form an important part of the vehicle's history. It's surprising how many sellers are happy to part with their car and accept your cash, but want to hang on to their photographs! In the latter event, you may be able to persuade the vendor to get a set of copies made.

**Note:** For export purposes a certificate of conformity may be required. Since 1998 every Morgan has been supplied with this document when delivered (in the UK or Europe). Certificates can get lost over time, but duplicates are available from Morgan at a cost of ●500 (at time of publication).

# 12 What's it worth?
– let your head rule your heart

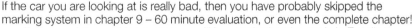

## Condition

If the car you are looking at is really bad, then you have probably skipped the marking system in chapter 9 – 60 minute evaluation, or even the complete chapter!

If you used the marking system, you'll know whether the car is in Excellent (maybe concours), Good, Average, or Poor condition or somewhere in-between these categories. You're now faced with the task of deciding what you're prepared to pay, and whether you're going to meet the asking price.

There is a wealth of information in various magazines, and on websites. The Morgan website car search is an excellent starting point, where you will see the prices asked for equivalent aged models. Look at your budget and see what is available within that budget. The Plus 8 keeps its value extremely well, so expected values tend to be known by vendors and purchasers alike.

The value of the car is determined by the package as a whole: colour, condition, extras and history. Magazine price guides are not really reliable due to the age ranges they cover and the fact that they do not take into account the range and cost of extras that can be fitted (potentially up to £12,000 on some examples). Morgans do not feature in the motor trade Cap 'black book' or Glasses guides.

Being a performance V8, occasional race versions may come up on the market.

This Plus 8 has a lot of interior extras, such as replacement steering wheel, door cards, console and uprated seats.

Wind deflectors and a folding windscreen kit are just some of the accessories added by owners.

These can be great buys if you also intend to do events and track days, as there is a good chance that a lot of expensive preparation has already been carried out. These should be treated separately to normal road cars.

Private sellers will ask about the same price as dealers, and in some cases more, as they believe their car is superior or they think they know the marketplace. You are not paying a premium at a dealer, you are paying for the security of knowing the car has been inspected, serviced, and supplied with a warranty. In addition, they can deal with a part-exchange and assist with finance if required. A private vendor will rarely offer any of the above. Auction houses may offer some of the features a dealer

Luggage racks are a popular option. This one has sidescreen storage.

can offer, but you'll need to check their terms. Based on this you should have more scope to negotiate with a private sale. Photographs of the car may give you clues to how long it's been on the market (summer/winter foliage in the background, for example).

Tastes change over time, green and red were the most popular colours up to the early 1990s, so it will be harder to find a blue example in this age range.

Minilite wheels, roll bar and engine upgrades: ideal for sprinting or track days.

## Desirable options/ extras

Every Morgan is different, and it depends on the look an owner has wanted to achieve. Some prefer a plain look, while others want nearly every option in the spec. The usual extras are: chrome/stainless wire wheels (although wires were not an option on the Plus 8 for decades), walnut dashboard, Moto-Lita steering wheel and luggage racks. There is also a massive range of other options and aftermarket accessories available.

Mesh grilles have become popular over recent years; with a little work they will fit earlier cars.

## Undesirable features

Homemade accessories or poorly fitted genuine accessories can spoil the car, both in looks and value. Buyers will often be deterred by a roll bar, assuming that it has been used on track or in competition. which may not be the case. Repaired insurance write-offs need to be carefully examined, and will never be worth top money.

## Striking a deal

There will only ever be a limited number of Plus 8s available, with limited editions being rare. Cars are now advertised to a worldwide audience, so you may need to be quick. Do not go to look at a car unless you are prepared to pay the asking price. Do not ask what the best price is before you have even viewed the car – this can give the impression that you are not a serious buyer. Private sellers tend to have a little more flexibility, dealers possibly less so. While negotiating the deal, consider what you might want to add to the car over the coming years. Additional optional extras fitted prior to collection could be a good area to haggle on. For example, the

dealer may be prepared to fit accessories within the asking price, or be prepared to split the costs for them. This can be a win:win situation, potentially helping the dealer secure a sale and you to save costs in the future.

35th anniversary back panel badge – but not all cars were badged.

Are you hands-on, and do you have plenty of free time? If so, that restoration project you have seen may be just the ticket. Rolling restorations allow you to concentrate on certain areas over a number of months/years – for example engine bay detailing one year, part retrim the next – allowing you to use the car in the interim. You'll pay more for one of these cars than one that needs a full restoration, but at least it will be together and basically roadworthy, although still in need of work.

A complete basket case or dismantled car will be a major undertaking requiring a lot of time, money and space. Labour will be the biggest factor, and is likely to take twice the number of hours you think. Budget between 200-400 hours to do a restoration well. A professional restorer or established Morgan dealer will be able to tackle the whole project for you. Be clear on what you want to achieve, though, and research and decide any upgrades before you get heavily involved in the work.

You may wish to go the DIY route, this has pros and cons. Either way you will be putting a car that deserves saving back on the road, but ensure what is done is done well. Attention to detail is key – wings cut in nicely, the correct type of fixings, number of fixings per panel, etc – otherwise a future buyer may have to strip it down and start again.

**Pros:** You can choose the colour and trim just like the new Morgan ordering experience. Morgans can change colours several times over their lifetimes, and it is not detrimental to the value. You'll gain new skills, meet great people whilst sourcing

Do not underestimate the amount of work and time required to repair a vehicle.

The axle has moved and there is wood frame damage under the panelwork on this 1986 Plus 8. The cost of repairing this was covered by insurance.

parts, and get huge satisfaction as the project comes together. As most parts are readily available, and given the nature of construction of a Plus 8, the project can come together quickly, with a limited range of tools.

**Cons:** Although built in a relatively simple way, you'll need to think several stages ahead to make the various components fit. Costly errors may only become noticeable later on. Don't paint the car until you know everything fits correctly. Mechanically, Plus 8s are relatively straightforward, but assembling the wood frame and doing panel work is a great skill. It may be wise to let Morgan experts tackle the more complex areas while you concentrate on other things to help manage/reduce costs. Overall the car will be better for it, and potentially worth more.

Don't cut corners. It is better to have the structure correct and then move on to the more visible items, which can be done over time.

I have seen some fantastic home restorations, and some shocking professional ones. Take photos and keep every invoice. In ten years' time they will be invaluable proof of the work undertaken.

Ask yourself, do you have the following: Time? Budget? Facilities? Expertise? And the big one: Patience?

# 14 Paint problems
– bad complexion, including dimples, pimples and bubbles

Cellulose paintwork was the standard finish until 1986, after which two-pack paint became standard, until 1998 when water-based paint was introduced. The car may have had paintwork repairs, so look for poor preparation and overspray. Look out for the following:

## Orange peel
This appears as an uneven paint surface, similar to the appearance of the skin of an orange. The fault is caused by the failure of atomised paint droplets to flow into each other when they hit the surface. It's sometimes possible to rub out the effect with proprietary paint cutting/rubbing compound or very fine grades of abrasive paper. A respray may be necessary in severe cases. Consult a bodywork repairer/paint shop for advice on the particular car.

An example of orange peel paintwork.

## Cracking
Severe cases are likely to have been caused by too heavy an application of paint (or filler beneath the paint). Also, insufficient stirring of the paint before application can lead to the components being improperly mixed, and cracking can result. Incompatibility with the paint already on the panel can have a similar effect. To rectify the problem it is necessary to rub down to a smooth, sound finish before respraying the problem area.

Cracking around headlamp pod.

## Crazing
Sometimes the paint takes on a crazed rather than a cracked appearance when the problems mentioned under 'Cracking' are present. This problem can also be caused by a reaction between the underlying surface and the paint. Paint removal and respraying the problem area is usually the only solution.

Crazing and blistering on a previous localised repair.

## Blistering

Almost always caused by corrosion of the metal beneath the paint. Usually perforation will be found in the metal and the damage will usually be worse than that suggested by the area of blistering. The metal will have to be repaired before repainting.

## Micro-blistering

Usually the result of an economy respray where inadequate heating has allowed moisture to settle on the car before spraying. Consult a paint specialist, but usually damaged paint will have to be removed before partial or full respraying. Can also be caused by car covers that don't 'breathe.'

## Fading

Some colours, especially reds, are prone to fading if subjected to strong sunlight for long periods without the benefit of polish protection. Sometimes proprietary paint restorers and/or paint cutting/rubbing compounds will retrieve the situation. Often a respray is the only real solution.

## Peeling

Often a problem with metallic paintwork when the sealing lacquer becomes damaged and begins to peel off. Poorly applied paint may also peel. The remedy is to strip and start again!

## Dimples

Dimples in the paintwork are caused by the residue of polish (particularly silicone types) not being removed properly before respraying. Paint removal and repainting is the only solution.

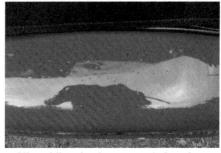

Micro-blistering is commonly found on bonnets and the back panel. This is on a rear wing.

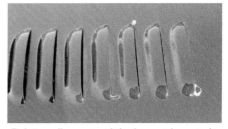

Paint peeling around the bonnet louvres is common on mid-1990s cars.

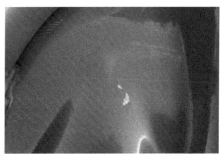

Front wing showing cracking, blistering and fading all within a small area.

## Dents

Small dents are usually easily cured by the 'Dentmaster,' or equivalent process, that sucks or pushes out the dent (as long as the paint surface is still intact). Companies offering dent removal services usually come to your home: consult a telephone directory or search online.

# 15 Problems due to lack of use

– just like their owners, Plus 8s need exercise!

Morgans, like humans, need regular exercise to keep in top condition. Ideally, Plus 8s need a run about ten miles every couple of weeks as a minimum. Winter storage and periods of very little use can cause problems.

## Seized components

Pistons in brake calipers, wheel, slave and master cylinders can all seize. Handbrakes, if left on, whether rod- or cable-operated, can seize (later cable- fitted cars are particularly prone to this). Later AP brake cylinders will seize through lack of use. Brake discs will go rusty and can cause juddering once the car is reused.

The clutch can seize if the friction plate becomes stuck to the flywheel because of corrosion. To free off the

Post-1993 wheel cylinders are prone to seizing if the car is left standing for long periods.

clutch try pumping the pedal, running the engine until normal running temperature is reached, and then trying the pedal may help.

## Fluids

Old acidic oil can corrode bearings. Check the colour of the engine: oil-light brown is a good sign, but black or thick black oil is a concern.

Uninhibited coolant can corrode internal waterways. Lack of antifreeze can cause core plugs to leak and even cracks in the block and cylinder head. Corrosion build up in the system will cause overheating.

Brake and clutch fluids absorb water from the atmosphere and should be renewed every two years. Old fluid with a high water content will cause components to seize and deteriorate. Brake failure can occur when the water turns to vapour as it comes into contact with hot brake components.

Clutch and brake master cylinder can fail due to lack of use and contaminated fluid, leaking into the footwell or failing altogether so the pedals have no resistance.

## Tyres

Tyres that have the weight of the car on them in a single position for a period of time will develop flat spots, resulting in vibration and steering shakes. The tyre walls become hard over time and will crack with age, or can blister (tyre bulges). Tyres should be changed regardless of condition if they are over ten years old.

The 14in alloy-wheeled cars are particularly prone to flat spotting. Later wheels are better, but can still cause a hard ride due to the hardness of the tyres.

*Tyres can flat-spot, causing severe vibrations through the steering.*

## Suspension
With lack of use, dampers can lose their elasticity or even seize. Suspension bushes dry out, particularly on the rear springs, causing squeaks and groans.
Front king pin bushes can seize, resulting in very little suspension movement and heavy steering.

## Rubber and plastic
Rubber hardens and cracks over time. Coolant hoses and fuel tank filler hoses can badly perish, swell and leak. Wiper blades harden and split. Plastics can discolour and become brittle.

*1976-on dashboard switches become brittle and are costly to replace.*

## Electrics
Batteries will be of little use if they have not been charged for several months, and use of battery conditioners can conceal problems. Earthing and grounding problems are common when connections have corroded, including those inside the car. Any multi-plug connection can corrode and may need cleaning and protection to avoid problems (eg, Vaseline or contact spray). Sparkplugs are liable to corrode in an unused engine, and wiring insulation can harden and fail.

Digital speedometers sometimes lose the mileage display. Storing in a dry warm cupboard may help the display to recover.

## Exhausts
Exhausts tend to be stainless nowadays, as older mild steel exhausts would have corroded by now. Factory exhausts became stainless as standard in 1997, but silencer boxes and catalytic converter flanges can corrode away.

## Weather equipment
Hoods should be stored fitted to the car as the material is likely to shrink. Damp conditions will quickly ruin weather equipment.

# 16 The Community

– key people, organisations and companies in the [model] world

Buying a Morgan is like extending your family. Help and assistance is always on hand, and the social scene is huge. Recommended contact points are:

## Morgan Motor Company

www.morgan-motor.co.uk
This is the home of Morgan where new cars are built. Use the website for more information on new cars, factory tours, accessories shop, locating used cars and links to the current dealer network throughout the world.

## Morgan Sports Cars Club

www.morgansportscarclub.com
For everything Morgan. Local area groups, club events, quality monthly magazine, and so much more.
Live outside the UK? 47 affiliated clubs are linked with the MSCC. Go to the website to find out more.

## Specialist insurance brokers

Morgan Insurance
Tel: 01420 594242
www.moginsurance.co.uk

Gott and Wynne
Tel: 01492 870991
www.gottandwynne.co.uk

Heritage Classic Car Insurance
Tel: 0121 248 9229
www.heritagecarinsurance.co.uk

## Motorsport specialists

Brands Hatch Morgans – www.morgan-cars.com
Richard Thorne Classic Cars – www.rtcc.co.uk
Revolutions – www.revolutions.uk.com
Techniques – www.techniques.uk.com
Williams Morgan – www.williamsautomotive.com

## Car accessories and upgrade suppliers

Morgan official dealers carry a good range of accessories and upgrades. They may specialise in a particular area or a range of extras for the Plus 8, so take a good look at what is available.

There are a number of independent suppliers who stock a range of vehicle accessories including exhausts, valances, dashboards, tuning upgrades, etc.

Librands  – www.librands.co.uk
Wolf Performance – www.wolfperformance.co.uk

Mulfab – www.mulfab.co.uk
Sifab – www.sifab.co.uk
Belmog – www.belmog.com
MK Holztechnik – www.mk-holztechnik.de
New Elms – www.newelms.com
Holden Vintage and Classic – www.holden.co.uk
GEE Ltd – https://geeltd.co.uk
Vintage Sheet Metal – www.morganspecialist.com

For Rover engine parts:
Rimmer Brothers – https://rimmerbros.com/
RPL Engineering – www.v8engines.com
John Earles – https://johnealesroverv8.co.uk

For gearbox and axle parts:
JB Sports Engineering – http://jb-engineering.co.uk

For Morgan interiors and hoods:
Allon White Sports Cars ltd – www.allonwhite.co.uk

Wheels:
Motor Wheel Services – http://www.mwsint.com

Steering wheels:
Moto Lita Ltd – www.moto-lita.co.uk

As I work for one of the main UK dealers it would be unfair of me to recommend particular dealers to buy from. To help you decide on a Plus 8, I would suggest starting with the car locator on the Morgan website, and then various classic car websites, where you will find some excellent specialists listed.

## Current UK and Channel Islands main dealers
Allon White Sports Cars – www.allonwhite.co.uk
Bell and Colvill – www.bellandcolvill.co.uk
Berrybrook – www.berrybrookmorgan.co.uk
Brands Hatch Morgans – www.morgan-kent.com
Jacksons – www..jacksonsci.com
Krazy Horse – www.krazyhorse.co.uk
Ledgerwood – www.ledgerwoodmorgan.co.uk
Melvyn Rutter – www.morgan-motors-cars.com
Morgan London – www.morgan-motor.com/london/
Morgan Works – www.morgan-motor.com/morgan-works-malvern/
Oakmere – www.oakmeremotorgroup.co.uk
Revolutions – www.revolutions.uk.com
Williams Morgan – www.williamsautomobiles.com

## Useful websites to find a used Morgan Plus 8
There are many other classic car sites, but these are continually being updated on a live basis. Some websites show old stock that may still be marked for sale, so call in

advance to ensure a particular car is still available. Some of the most popular sites in the UK are:

www.carandclassic.co.uk
www.pistonheads.com
www.classiccarsforsale.co.uk
www.autotrader.co.uk

## Useful reference books/magazines

*Original Morgan.* John Worrall and Liz Turner. Motorbooks International, ISBN 9780760316443.
*Making a Morgan.* Andreas Hensing. Veloce Publishing, ISBN 9781787113695.
*Morgan 100 years.* Charles Morgan and Gregory Houston Bowden. Michael O'Mara, ISBN 978-1843172673.
*MOG* magazine. Alpha Publishing, tel: 01905 611926.

Note: A workshop manual is not available for any of the Plus 8s. The last manual produced was for Morgan Four 1936-1981 by Brooklands Books. There are various other car and classic car magazines available in most countries, many run special features on Morgans on a regular basis.

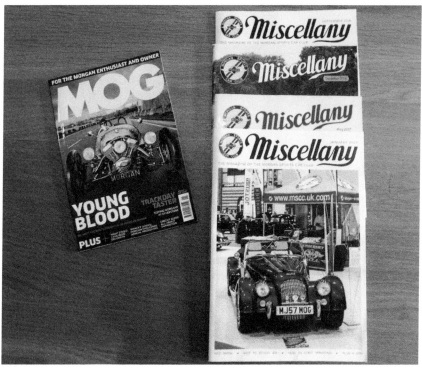

Club and dedicated magazines provide extra information and details of events.

# 17 Vital statistics
– essential data at your fingertips

All Morgans are made at Pickersleigh Road, Malvern Link, Worcester WR14 2LL.
Key features of the limited editions have been included.

## Plus 8 3.5 Moss gearbox 1968-1972

| Engine capacity | Bhp | Gearbox | Fuel system type |
| --- | --- | --- | --- |
| 3528cc | 160 | Moss four-speed | SU HS6 carburettors |

All chassis numbers start with an R until 1998, starting with R7000. An aluminium
body was offered as an option from 1969. Crash padding was added to the top of
the dashboard from 1971.

## Plus 8 coupé
The only traditional factory-built automatic gearbox Plus 8. Built in 1971 for Mrs
Jane Morgan. The car is part of the Morgan factory collection.

## Plus 8 3.5 Rover gearbox 1972-1976

| Engine capacity | Bhp | Gearbox | Fuel system type |
| --- | --- | --- | --- |
| 3528 cc | 143 | Rover four-speed | SU H1 F6 carburettors |

Chassis width increased, with body and wings to suit, from October 1973

## Plus 8 four-seater
Built for Eric White of Allon White & Son Ltd  in 1972. This is the only factory-built
Plus 8 four-seater, and was finished in Westminster green. The car is now in private
ownership.

## Plus 8 lightweight (1975-1977)
Mechanically as above. Only 19 were produced, featuring an aluminium body,
aluminium plate front floorboards, and Milrace 14in wheels painted black with slots
outlined in silver. Despite the four-speed gearbox, it had a wider five-speed body.
These are now incredibly rare.

## Plus 8 3.5 five-speed gearbox 14in wheels  1977-1982

| Engine capacity | Bhp | Gearbox | Fuel system type |
| --- | --- | --- | --- |
| 3528 | 155 | Rover LT77 Five-speed | SU carburettors until 1981. Stromberg CD175s fitted from 1981. |

Anodised aluminium bumpers were fitted, and the body width increased.

## Plus 8 3.5 five-speed 15in alloy wheel 1982-1987

| Engine capacity | Bhp | Gearbox | Fuel system type |
|---|---|---|---|
| 3528 cc | 155; 190 (injection models) | Rover LT77 five-speed | Strombergs until 1983, when Lucas LE fuel-injection was offered as an option until 1987 |

Rack and pinion steering was offered as an option in 1984, becoming standard in 1985. Walnut dashboards became an option from 1986.

Wings-off two-pack paintwork was introduced, and the wood frame was treated from 1986, although some earlier cars had factory-treated wood frames from 1984.

## Plus 8 3.5 five-speed injection 1984-1990

| Engine capacity | Bhp | Gearbox | Fuel system type |
|---|---|---|---|
| 3528cc | 190 | Rover LT77 five-speed | Lucas LE fuel-injection |

A galvanised chassis was offered from 1989. Bhp can vary depending on exhaust type.

## Plus 8 3.9 1990-1997

| Engine capacity | Bhp | Gearbox | Fuel system type |
|---|---|---|---|
| 3946cc | 190 | Rover LT77 five-speed; Rover R380 fitted from 1994 | Lucas 14CUX |

Telescopic rear shock absorbers were fitted from 1992. There was a chrome wire wheel option from March 1993. The rear saddle frame design was changed and the lower middle crossmember position was moved to allow for extra seat movement in 1994. Stainless steel exhausts became standard from 1997. Bhp can vary depending on exhaust type.

## Plus 8 4.6 1996-2001

| Engine capacity | Bhp | Gearbox | Fuel system type |
|---|---|---|---|
| 4555cc | 217 | R380 five-speed | Lucas 14CUX |

Used 3.9 engine management system on the Rover 4.6 block. There was an option of 16in centre lock alloy wheels. The first few cars were short-door models, most were long-door models.

## Plus 8 3.9 1997-2001 long door

| Engine capacity | Bhp | Gearbox | Fuel system type |
|---|---|---|---|
| 3946cc | 190 | R380 five-speed | Lucas 14CUX; Lucas-Sagem GEMS from 1998 (US), and from 2001 in Europe |

114 changes were made to the car for it to comply with European regulations in 1998, including a full Certificate of Conformity. 17-digit chassis numbers were introduced in 1998, with the last five numbers being the car number. The oiler valve system was removed in 2000, and manufacturer warranty changed to two years from 2001.

## Plus 8 4.0 2001-2004

| Engine capacity | Bhp | Gearbox | Fuel system type |
|---|---|---|---|
| 3946cc | 190 | Rover R380 | Lucas-SAGEM GEMS |

Engine changed to the 4.0-litre Federal engine across all markets. The hood changed to two bars instead of three in 2002, the Morgan 20-second easy-fit hood was introduced from 2003. Overriders were optional from 2003. Not all cars towards the end of production were badged as 35th anniversary models.

## Plus 8 Le Mans 62 edition 2002

| Engine capacity | Bhp | Gearbox | Fuel system type |
|---|---|---|---|
| 3946cc | 190 | Rover R380 | Lucas-SAGEM GEMS |

Only 40 4/4s and 40 Plus 8s were produced, in Le Mans green with a cream hard top, unique dash and floor mats. It had a driver's door handle only, 16in stainless wire wheels and overriders, and every car came with a signed picture.

## Plus 8 35th Anniversary 2003-2004

| Engine capacity | Bhp | Gearbox | Fuel system type |
|---|---|---|---|
| 3946cc | 190 | Rover R380 | Lucas-SAGEM GEMS |

Customers could choose from the standard option list items; however, any colour leather and paintwork colour, including metallic were included (saving £2000 off list prices at the time). Le Mans 16in wire wheels were available and a unique 35th anniversary rear badge. This model was phased out and replaced by the Roadster later in 2004.

**More from the Essential Buyer's Guide series**

Having one of these books in your pocket is just like having a real marque expert by your side. Benefit from Phil Benfield's years of Morgan experience, learn how to spot a bad car quickly and how to assess a promising one like a professional. Get the right car at the right price!

ISBN: 978-1-787115-58-3
Paperback • 19.5x13.9cm
• 96 pages • 97 colour pictures

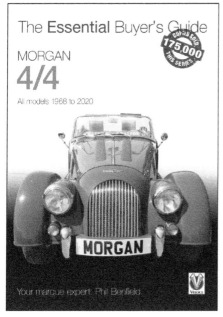

ISBN: 978-1-787117-26-6
Paperback • 19.5x13.9cm
• 96 pages • 119 colour pictures

For more information and price details, visit our website at
www.veloce.co.uk
• email: info@veloce.co.uk
• Tel: +44(0)1305 260068

The Essential Buyer's Guide™ series ...

For more details visit:
www.veloce.co.uk
email: info@veloce.co.uk
tel: 01305 260068